GW00771004

GEOFF WILLIAMS'
AYLESBURY LNWR
Researching and Modelling the Prototype

GEOFFREY WILLIAMS
1913-1998

This view of Aylesbury dates from *c.*1913/14 and is from a rare lantern slide which was discovered in 2018. Geoff would have been fascinated and thrilled to see it as it contains valuable historic period detail.

As well as giving a clear view of the station glass roof internal framing it interestingly shows a smoke trough through the glass at the outer end. Smoke troughs had been removed by the time Geoff 'found' the station in 1955, but from contemporary descriptions he added them to his model at the buffer stop end. This would be logical as the engine would be underneath them when the train arrived. Before this photograph surfaced it was not known that smoke troughs were also fitted at the other end. The hanging gas lamp is of LNWR standard pattern and the same as those fitted along the platform fence where they were fitted onto vertical cast iron posts with two curved supports picking up the same side fittings as in this picture. The engine must be stopped very close to the buffer stop as the first station sign, 'General / Waiting Room', was the first room past the booking office. The next room had the sign 'Ladies / Second and Third Class / Waiting Room'. Note the very low platform.

The locomotive, Coal Tank No. 1054, was built in 1888 and later became LMS No. 7799 and BR No. 58926 and was the last Coal Tank to be withdrawn in 1958. It was subsequently preserved and can still be seen running as restored to its LNWR condition. It is the condition of the loco that helps date this photo as *c.*1913/1914 as it has a modified whistle without a top 'acorn' (after 1909) and a drip strip has not yet been fitted along the cab roof side (from *c.*1913). The condition suggests it is just 'ex-Works'. The first three carriages are 32ft 0in six-wheelers from the 1880s, cascaded to branch line use and are probably working as the branch set at the time of the photograph. This fits with the description of the formation of the set at that time by George Thorne (see below). The end vehicle on the train is a mystery as it doesn't seem to conform to any LNWR profile. It could possibly be a covered carriage truck or horse box but looks too wide to be one of these.

The gentleman on the far left is George Thorne (see p. 55). Born in 1887, George was the passenger guard on the branch from around 1912, having started working in the bookstall there when he was too young for railway service. He was still passenger guard on the branch on the last passenger train on 31st January 1953 (see also photograph on page 102 of Bill Simpson's book *The Aylesbury Railway*) and then transferred to Aylesbury Town station until he retired after 49½ years' railway service. Geoff met him *c.*1957 and got to know him well and attended his funeral in 1961. George was the main source of information for Geoff in his early research into the branch. Standing next to George Thorne is probably porter Arthur Clarke (see p. 73). Geoff acquired photographs of both taken *c.*1912 which were taken by porter Billy Sutton and it is possible that Billy may be the third of the three station staff but no previous photographs have been identified to confirm.

Bob Williams collection, with added locomotive information from Peter Skellon

© Wild Swan Books Ltd. and the author 2021
ISBN 978-1-912038-64-0

WILD SWAN BOOKS LTD.

Designed by Stephen Phillips. Printed by Elgar Books Ltd.

Published by
WILD SWAN BOOKS LTD.
4 Tollbridge Studios, Toll Bridge Road, Bath BA1 7DE

GEOFF WILLIAMS'

AYLESBURY LNWR
Researching and Modelling the Prototype

by BOB WILLIAMS

Geoff Williams first discovered Aylesbury (LNWR) station in 1955 and was immediately drawn to its potential as a model of a real prototype. At the time many of the original LNWR features including the glass station screen were still present, although passenger services had ended in 1953. Thus began Geoff's lifelong interest in the station, involving extensive historical research, on-site surveys and recording before the station was demolished in the mid-1960s, culminating in the finescale 4mm EM model which survives today. Geoff built two Aylesbury models. The first, Aylesbury Mark 1, was started in the late-1950s, but as Geoff's modelling skills and historical knowledge of the prototype improved he decided to make a fresh start. Aylesbury Mark 1 was sold in the early 1960s and, following a move in 1963 to a new house with a large loft in which to permanently house the model, work on the improved Aylesbury Mark 2 began in earnest in 1964. Geoff worked on his model and research continuously until his passing in 1998, after which the model was carefully dismantled and stored by Geoff's family. The layout is today in the care of the Risborough & District Model Railway Club, and remains a testament to Geoff's careful observation of the prototype and dedicated painstaking modelling over four decades.   *Photograph by Andy York, BRM magazine*

CONTENTS

Geoff Williams' Aylesbury LNWR, the culmination of over forty years of research and modelling.   *Photograph by Andy York, BRM magazine*

FOREWORD

I am both pleased and honoured to be asked by Bob to write this foreword to a book dedicated to the work of his father, Geoff Williams. Such commitment to the re-creation of the LNWR Aylesbury branch was an inspiration to me and to many other people. His enthusiasm was matched only by his keenness to help and encourage others in whatever they were doing.

He was born in the year 1913, so was able to remember the LNWR before its demise, and was pleased he could say that he was born in the same year in which the first of the iconic Claughton Class of locomotives were built.

Apart from one earlier layout, he had the foresight to concentrate all his efforts on this single prototype and from 1955 until his death in 1998, his work culminated in a stunning layout, acutely portrayed.

On the way, he amassed mountains of documents, drawings and photographs to help him build up an accurate depiction of his subject, and in his own way, was leading the way in research techniques.

This dedication to one prototype is in stark contrast to many other modellers, myself included, who never can quite settle on the perfect project. Once the final version of the layout had been defined and the majority of the work was done, there were still parts of the project where Geoff had to wait for technology to catch up with his expectations, and this wait was not a patient one! He was anxious to build an important element of the layout, the footbridge, but it was only with the advent of the process of etching sheet metal from both sides that this could come about. With the guidance of Colin Waite, the finest exponent of etched components at the time, Geoff was able to prepare the hand-drawn artwork and Colin was able to get the parts etched.

Following my first visit to Geoff's home in Cuffley, I asked him if I could build him a carriage as a way of saying thanks, using parts moulded in styrene sheet, produced in collaboration with the kit manufacturer, Roxey Mouldings. This short-lived process was another faltering step along the path that took us towards the fully detailed etched brass kits we are now used to. I am glad to say that Geoff was delighted by the results and I am equally pleased to say that one of my vehicles was running on Aylesbury.

With the footbridge problem solved, Geoff had just one large hole to fill on the layout and this was the gas works. This part of the project was important to Geoff, as he was involved in the gas industry throughout his working life. Eventually this missing piece in the jigsaw was complete and it remains today as a wonderful example of skillful and accurate modelling.

With their interest in researching into the LNWR, both Geoff and Bob attended the inaugural meeting of the London & North Western Railway Society. However, Geoff did not join until a couple of years later, becoming member No. 127. He served as the Secretary of the L&NWRS for a number of years.

It is very gratifying to know that Aylesbury still lives on and has been sympathetically restored by members of the Risborough & District Model Railway Club. Their aim is to be able to exhibit the layout to the public so that many more people will be able to experience Geoff's wonderful creation at first hand.

It is a fitting and lasting legacy to Geoff's memory and a tribute to his dedication and modelling skills.

MIKE PEASCOD
Pinner, November 2020

INTRODUCTION

This book, written nearly twenty years after he died, tells the story of how Geoff's interest in railways began and how it followed him through his life and resulted, eventually, in his 4mm scale EM gauge model of Aylesbury High Street station. In the first part it can be seen how his interest developed and also how some of his modelling methods reflected his approach to real life situations. It discusses how he developed some of his modelling techniques and tells how Aylesbury EM became known to modellers. Some of the modelling short cuts are also revealed as well as the many people who encouraged and influenced him throughout his modelling period. The illustrations to this part are mainly of the model. Photographs are credited where possible but it is regretted that there are several where the identity of the photographer is unknown.

Part two looks at Aylesbury and how he researched the area ready to build the model. This includes his visits to the town, details of the local people he met as well as the various photographs and sketches he made himself, many of which are reproduced to illustrate this part of the book. Photos in this part not taken by Geoff are credited as appropriate with uncredited photos being taken by him. In many cases his research went outside the railway boundary to enable him to construct a reasonably accurate backscene to the model and this has resulted in the model providing a record of what some of Aylesbury was like in pre-WWi days and also later. Today computers enable much of this research to be done from the comfort of a chair at home, with references being available through websites like Karl Vaughan's excellent 'Aylesbury Remembered' Facebook page, which does now include some of Geoff's photographs. However, Geoff never had a computer.

Geoff was an active member of the LNWR Society, as are sons Bob and Mike, and attended the inaugural meeting in 1973. He was Society Secretary from 1982 to 1988, was made a Vice-President in 1989 and was President from 1993 until his death in 1998. His sons have continued to build on his research into the Aylesbury Branch and some of the illustrations in this book have been acquired since his death. It is hoped he would have been proud and excited by the family's continued interest.

Many people have contributed to Geoff's research over the years and these are credited where appropriate but special thanks are also due to Stephen Phillips for converting many of Geoff's sketches into the beautiful drawings included in the book.

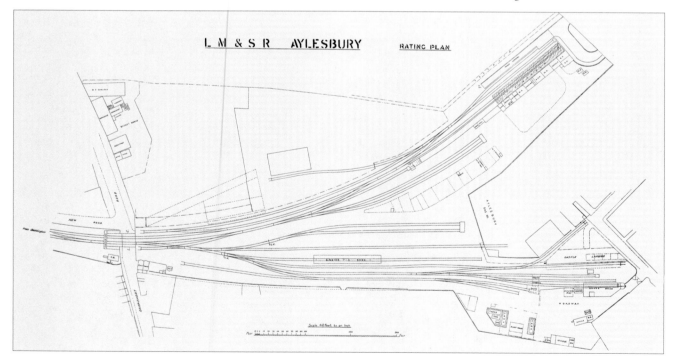

LM&SR Rating Plan showing the layout of Aylesbury Station *c*.1943. The siding upper centre was not present during the LNWR period and was added when the council took over the former basket works site *c*.1930.
LNWR Society Archives, ref DPLAN0597

PART ONE

Geoff Williams and the evolution of Aylesbury LNWR

Geoffrey Williams was born in Tottenham, North London on 14th April 1913 (almost exactly a year after the *Titanic* disaster) but even from an early age he had an interest in railways despite having no encouragement from his immediate family. He had one much older brother who had no interest in railways at all and was in the Army. The young Geoff started with model trains quite early, encouraged by an uncle, and these were usually large scale on the kitchen scullery floor. The family later moved to Sidney Avenue, Palmers Green, still in Great Eastern Railway territory, where his memories were mainly of 'Buckjumpers' and the 'Jazz Trains'. However, these were basically to satisfy the commuter traffic into London. It was Euston that fired his imagination where the trains were longer with the wonderful LNWR plum and spilt milk livery but, more importantly, they went to exotic-sounding places like Crewe, Holyhead and Carlisle. Although the Grouping came when he was only ten he knew LNWR livery well and took a keen enough interest to see his first 'Tishy' (Walschaerts valve gear 4-6-0 but with inside cylinders) arrive on a train at Euston and think that it had suffered an accident and the outside cylinders been knocked off!

Geoff with his first model railway in the garden of the Tottenham home in 1919. The four-wheeled engine and tender by Bing was, of course, LNWR.

Geoff's model railway in the 1920s. A poor photograph showing a Hornby 4-4-0 converted to an 0-4-4 Tank. The wagons were built from kits by Milbro and LMC.

Leaving school, Geoff started working in the garage of the Tottenham District Light, Heat and Power Company (later part of Eastern Gas) where his father was company secretary and developed an interest in all things mechanical which soon led to motorbikes which he loved to dismantle, rebuild and improve. As girlfriends soon followed the motorbikes it seemed his interest in railways was left in the past. He started riding motorbikes competitively and did several rallies around the UK, winning an award at one of them. With a small circle of motorcycle chums he then started to venture abroad and in 1939 decided on a holiday touring Germany with friends on motorbikes. It was during this holiday that war was declared and he considered he was lucky to make it back to the UK. This was during his holiday from work of course as by then he was working for Eastern Gas on gas production sites. He was to continue to work for Eastern Gas for the rest of his working life, eventually retiring as a site engineer responsible for building gas holders and associated plant over much of eastern England after approaching fifty years' service.

During the war Geoff met his future wife, Beryl, who was ten years his junior and worked for the bank. They married during the war but shortly after came his call up papers and he joined the Royal Navy where he worked mainly on mine sweepers. The only action he saw was when a British merchant ship hit a mine in British waters. Back from the war the couple looked for a house, which was far from easy in those days. He was fortunate to find an end of terrace house in Cheshunt

which was occupied by two old ladies as well, although neither lived for long afterwards. The downside was that it was just seven doors away from his in-laws. It cost the grand sum of £900 but that was during war time!

In January 1949 their first son, Bob, was born and the motorbike had to be fitted with a sidecar. Geoff soon realised this would not be practical as the family grew larger and he bought a car. He built a garage for the motorbike and sidecar at the back of the terraced house out of angle iron and asbestos sheets which were sawn up on the back lawn. The garage was distinguished in having a large circular window in one door and was still standing over sixty-five years later. This was no doubt due to Geoff's tendency to over-engineer things he built, which was to pay off later in his model railway endeavours. Although the garage was intended to house just his motorbike and sidecar by the time the family moved from Cheshunt in the early 1960s it was still big enough to take his Standard Vanguard – just!

As Bob grew up and was joined by a brother, Pete, in 1953, so Geoff's interest in railways returned and he soon started building a freelance model on a board. This was 16.5mm gauge and loosely LMS-based and included some LMS non-corridor carriages (from Hamblings) and a Reidpath 4F which was very heavy and, with a flywheel in the cab, a very smooth runner. The layout itself was not very practical as it had a steep gradient along one side and some sharp curves and soon he started looking for ideas to start again.

A return to model railways in the 1950s resulted in this 16.5mm gauge LMS-based layout. The carriages were by Hamblings and the LMS 4F by Reidpath, with track from PECO. The one in twenty gradient on the left and 18in radius curves were not very practical. *Geoff Williams 1953/4*

The 1950s layout viewed across the goods shed accentuates the steep incline along one side. The Hornby Duchess was on loan from a neighbour. *Geoff Williams 1953/4*

DISCOVERING AYLESBURY STATION 1955

Geoff's job took him all over the Eastern Gas area but sometimes after work he would explore railway stations on his way home. One day in 1955 he stumbled into Southern Gas territory and found Aylesbury High Street station which had closed to passenger traffic just two years before, although a goods service was still running. He was struck by what an attractive compact station it was. It still retained many LNWR period features including the station building with glass screen and roof, LNWR signals and signal box, level crossing, engine shed and lots more. This was the first of probably over forty visits to Aylesbury station over the next seventeen years to meticulously photograph, measure and sketch as much of it as he could and a 4mm scale model was begun almost immediately.

AYLESBURY MARK 1

Geoff had been impressed by the improved look and running of EM (18mm) over 16.5mm gauge, mainly on layouts he had seen at the Model Railway Club's Easter exhibition at Central Hall Westminster, and the new model was to EM from the start. He joined the EM Gauge Society and often bought parts from Doug Fairhurst in Enfield not far from home. The terraced house had just a lounge, dining room and kitchen downstairs but after the wall between the lounge and dining room was removed the layout, on four six-foot boards about a foot wide, was designed to fit on end behind a curtain beside one of the lounge chimney breasts. When erected it went from the lounge window through to almost the dining window. The

third board had an arc cut out of it to allow for the dining room door to be opened but even then all visitors had to duck under the model which was perhaps four feet high to make this easier. This was acceptable to railway enthusiasts but not so good when the vicar called! Each board was quite narrow and you can imagine Geoff's dismay when a later visit to Aylesbury showed that there were a lot more sidings and a goods shed behind the locomotive shed that he had not seen before. This he decided to add in low relief in a very simplified form.

The faithful Reidpath 4F was converted to EM and was the first loco on the new model. Because of all the LNWR features still in place at Aylesbury Geoff decided to set the model in the pre-group era so the next loco was to be a Webb 2-4-0 Chopper Tank. Thanks to his practical engineering experience in the past he decided to scratchbuild, buying in just the motor, gears, wheels and buffers. He made everything else using nickel silver sheet for the body, which he believed soldered better, and brass for the chassis. Ross Pochin was a strong influence here as Geoff had admired his 7mm scale Chopper Tank at an MRC show and Ross even gave him several drawings and a couple of photographs. He also discussed Chopper Tanks with the S-gauge modeller Stan Garlick. Geoff was not really well equipped to scratchbuild an engine as he had no workshop or lathe at the time, just a lot of patience and determination. The boiler mountings were 'turned' using files in a Wolf electric drill held against the bench in the garage. It is believed the wheels were early K's brass and the motor and flywheel were certainly K's. However, the finished model, painted and lined by Geoff, performed really well.

A goods train posing in front of Norfolk Terrace on Aylesbury Mark 1. Note the much cruder trackwork. The K's Coal Tank No. 2357 was also quite basic with no brakes and flangeless centre coupled wheels and was sold with the layout. This photo also shows the Diagram 45 meat van in the original incorrect white livery that was to be changed following discussion with Jim Richards. Apart from rolling stock none of Aylesbury Mark 1 was transferred to Mark 2, Norfolk Terrace then having to be made again. The timber merchant's lorry was a Lesney 'Models of Yesteryear' AEC 'Y' type, repainted in a fictitious livery as no other details were known at the time, *c.*1959. By 1960 Geoff had discovered the name of the timber merchant, Mr Richards, and the lorry was subsequently re-lettered. *Ray Kinsey*

It was probably the difficulty of effectively building a 4mm scale engine in the garage and from discussion with many acquaintances at the Easter MRC shows that Geoff decided he needed a workshop, and a brick-built shed with corrugated asbestos roof was then built at the bottom of the garden. This made the building of his next scratchbuilt engine much easier and he completed his Webb 5ft 6in 2-4-2 Tank using similar principles to the Chopper. However, although the brick shed was very warm in summer as it faced south, it was very cold in winter. A portable two-bar electric fire was bought for the winter and this stood on the floor in one corner but had the drawback that it was easy to get carried away modelling while the fire singed the hairs off one leg! Bob spent countless happy hours standing watching beside his father and this experience no doubt led to him following his father's interest.

Bob, and later Pete, would sometimes accompany Geoff to Aylesbury for more research and both were sometimes included in photographs Geoff took of the station. Now although the station was still open for goods traffic Geoff and his sons used to walk around the whole site taking photographs and notes. On one occasion they were walking around the engine shed when a voice said 'What are you doing there?' That was when Geoff met George Thorne who was then coming up to retirement but had started work at Aylesbury station before the First war. This proved a very important turning point in collecting information about the branch as George introduced him to other old ex-employees and he also had an amazing memory himself, but we will come to that later.

From then on research about Aylesbury was along two lines. One was general research to gather any information to build a picture of the branch while the other was specific research to answer a question encountered in building the model. As information grew Geoff became more aware of the shortcomings of his model, and this came to a head when he found that the glue he had used to stick down some of the track had shrunk and caused the fibre sleepers to arch their backs thus widening the gauge. The gauge widening had an unexpected benefit though as it was found the trains ran more easily on those parts of the model so affected.

This together with Geoff's expanding historical knowledge of the prototype prompted his decision to start again with a completely new model of Aylesbury.

The passenger platform of Aylesbury Mark 1. Note the very low-relief gas works in the background, *c.*1959. *Ray Kinsey*

Aylesbury Mark 1 showing Geoff's second scratchbuilt locomotive 5ft 6in Tank No. 910. Geoff rebuilt the chassis with split frames and installed a larger K's motor and flywheel *c.*1960 to give the engine more pulling power. The carriage is a Ratio wooden 50ft suburban with the panelling painted on.
Ray Kinsey

AYLESBURY MARK 2 – A FRESH START

Geoff built the first two baseboards from ¾in block board on 2in × 1in framing, all two feet wide. The whole board was covered in cork sheet but, remembering Geoff's over-engineering principle of pre-war days, the track was much more substantial. This time he used 'TT' flat-bottomed rail (no finescale bullhead rail was then available) laid to a gauge of 18.2mm, to benefit from his earlier experience. The sleepers were plywood from the EM Gauge Society with each sleeper having two brass rivets, riveted over and filed flat. Sleepers were then stuck down to the cork with Araldite and a piece of 2in × 1in timber shaped like a punt with emery paper stuck to it run over them all to ensure they were all level. The rails were then soldered to every brass rivet and adjusted by eye to ensure good alignment using a roller gauge for the second rail. The result was solid, beautifully aligned and ran well but looked wrong being flat-bottomed rail so blobs of Polyfilla were put on every 'chair' on the outside only to allow for running stock without finescale flanges. When dry the emery punt was run along at 45 degrees and then every 'chair' cut to shape and secured with a dab of shellac each side. Rail and chairs then had to be painted. This was a very long job but the results have caused little problem in fifty-five years.

As Aylesbury Mark Two advanced so it became clear that he needed to dispose of Mark One which had become well known through some magazine articles in *Model Railway News* and the several visitors who had seen it. It was advertised

for sale and bought by Pat Whitehouse, of TV's 'Railway Roundabout' fame. Pat never visited the house himself but sent a man with a van down from Birmingham to collect the layout and a small selection of stock Geoff sold with it. It was sold intact with nothing moved over to Mark Two but features like the footbridge had never been completed. A few months later Mark One did appear at the end of one of the 'Railway Roundabout' TV programmes, including a rather nice model of a Prince of Wales 4-6-0, built by J. P. (Jim) Richards. It was seen at Tyseley a few years later and is believed to still exist at the date of writing.

The typically-LNWR station glass roof and screen presented a challenge as, although he believed the screen was built from muranese (obscured) glass he wanted it clear so as not to hide detail in the station building and on the platform. The steel frame structure for the glass roof was also quite complex and was very visible as it was mainly built externally above the glass. The entire steelwork was therefore made from soldered brass sections, the resulting structure being another of Geoff's over-engineered models, probably being strong enough to stand on! The station building itself was quite a large model and was built to scale length over thirty inches long (the platform itself was about six inches short of scale). With no suitable Plastikard available in those days, it was built from a good quality brick-embossed English bond card made by Ballard Bros of Birmingham. This was hand-coloured to match Geoff's observation of the building as he had seen it.

Aylesbury Mark 2

A view of Aylesbury High Street from the station. Note the North and Randall premises opposite built using help from the company. The chalk sketches on the right show preparation for further buildings along the High Street which were then in progress. The view also shows clearly the steel structure over the glass station roof which is built from soldered brass sections.

Photo c.1971

Looking down on the completed Aylesbury High Street scene including the Chandos Hotel on the corner. The other side of the coal yard wall is the gas company premises with the gas manager's house.

The scene on the horse and carriage dock. The cars are plastic 'Replicars' models from Harbutt's.

The station screen showing colourful flower beds and hanging baskets. The hanging baskets are made of brass with the supports soldered on, passed through a hole through the middle and bent down to represent trailing plants. *Photo P. J. Kelley c.1971*

A cruel enlargement of a photo taken through the entrance door at the end of the platform. Note the typical LNWR roof brackets.

George the Fifth No. 2495 *Bassethound* on a train of parcels and milk vans. Gas works not yet built, *c.*1971. *P. J. Kelley*

The platform lamps were turned in Perspex. Geoff never saw the original LNWR elevated ground frame which he modelled from information obtained following much discussion with former staff who had known the branch in earlier days. The Bovril advertisement is an old Bassett-Lowke tinplate sign. Elsewhere Geoff carefully hand lettered signs to achieve the correct period atmosphere. *Photo P. J. Kelley c.1971*

A NEW HOME – DECEMBER 1963

Not long after this the family moved to a detached house in Cuffley and for a while modelling took a back seat.

Geoff always insisted that the loft in the Cuffley house played no part in his decision to buy it but it <u>was</u> ideal for a model railway. The house was built in 1938 with a high pitched roof and a gable at each end. This gave a floorboarded loft space that could be stood up in thirty-four feet long by eight feet wide with a brick chimney passing through about ten feet from one end and just a few very large structural roof timbers, unlike the multitude of smaller timbers found in more recent houses. One of the large cross members (a collar) in particular was 'in the way' so, after seeking advice Geoff introduced extra bracing down to the floor and then removed the one beam. The roof moved in enough to nip the saw but measurements before and after confirmed the roof had only moved by the thickness of the saw. He decided to mount the model on top of the main roof timbers (collars) spanning on 2 × 2in angle iron. This made the railway four feet eight and a half inches from the floor (how appropriate but coincidental!) which made for a good viewing height, apart from children(!), but also meant that working on wiring etc. could be done from sitting on a chair beneath. The roof itself was lined with polythene sheet stapled to the rafters (to stop dust) with large polystyrene tiles fitted to that using battens (for insulation). The result was that little dust settled on the model and the temperature did not vary dramatically throughout the year. A window was fitted to one gable end and an extractor fan to the other which ventilated and freshened the air when there were several visitors

or if it had become stale with lack of use.

Access to the loft was initially the usual 'stand on the kitchen steps and jump the last bit' but this was obviously not acceptable when carrying models or for visitors coming to view the layout. A single ladder was then made, leaning at about five degrees off vertical, and hinged just below the trap door to the loft. So as to avoid it becoming an obstacle to normal household movement, Geoff designed a method to winch it up against the ceiling using pulleys and ropes, the ladder being secured in the ceiling position by winding the rope around a cleat fixed to the wall.

The railway area of the loft was separated from normal loft storage by vertical hardboard walls with doors into the loft areas for suitcases, old wallpaper, etc. The railway itself had a hardboard fascia board painted black about twelve inches deep, below which was hung a black curtain down to the floor. Hanging down from the roof apex to within about eighteen inches of the model was a hardboard screen behind which were 5ft strip lights to try to give hidden lighting which approximated to daylight for the layout. This worked well for visitors but the upper screen sometimes got in the way for maintenance, especially on wider parts of the model. A few strategically placed relics were placed on the visitor side of the layout, most of which had an Aylesbury Branch connection. One of these was a fogman's bell from Cheddington signal box which was linked to a push-button in the lounge downstairs and was essential to alert those in the loft, carried away with model railway talk, that tea was ready downstairs.

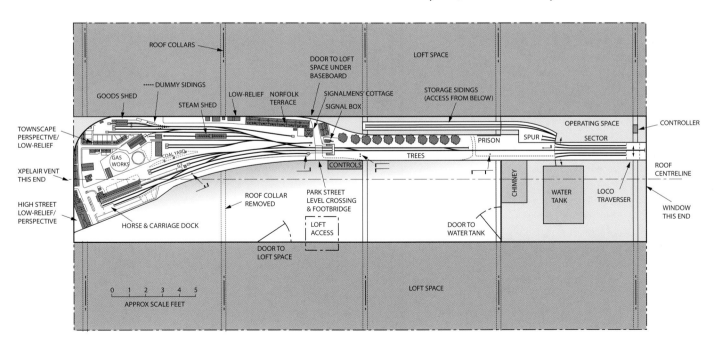

Plan of the loft at Cuffley which Geoff adapted to permanently house his model. The room available measured 34ft × 8ft. Access to the sector plate was by ducking under the baseboard by the chimney. Geoff fitted a window at one end, with an Xpelair extractor fan at the other to aid ventilation.

The loft setting

A general view of the layout in its loft setting. The genuine LNWR block instrument was wired to a similar one at the Cheddington (fiddle yard) end. The lamp fixed to the house chimney was from Marston Gate station and the two oval cast iron plates below were house number plates from the Aylesbury signalmen's cottages. Although the ceiling light bulb is on to illuminate the loft for the photograph, this would normally have been turned off so the only lighting was by three 5ft strip lights over the model concealed behind the hanging white screen. The black hardboard fascia protruded down about a foot in front of the baseboard and below it was a black curtain almost to the floor to bring the focus onto just the model itself.

Another angle of the viewing area in the Cuffley loft. Note the imitation carriage panelling on the right. Other Aylesbury items were the passenger starter signal arm, the LNWR Loco Crane No. 5 cast iron plate from a crane at Aylesbury and, in the top right hand corner, the Aylesbury staff and sample ticket necessary for single line working.

Photographs P. J. Kelley c.1971

Publisher's note

* The use of expanded polystyrene insulation was common in the 1960s, but would not meet present day building and fire regulations which should be complied with. Consideration must also be given to floor loading and fire escape access/egress. Removal/alteration of structural roof timbers should not be attempted without consulting a qualified structural engineer.

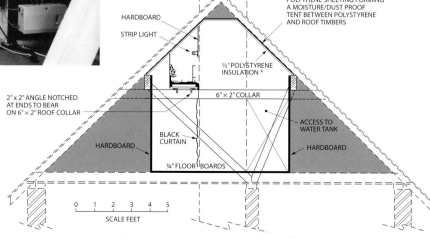

Cross-section through the loft at Cuffley.

ESTABLISHING THE NEW LAYOUT

The first two existing baseboards from the previous house were retained but the beginnings of baseboard three were rejected and a new baseboard perhaps fourteen feet long was made for the simple straight track section to just past the chimney. Beyond the chimney was the fiddle yard. This separate baseboard about 6ft 6in long was entirely painted matt black to try to make it unobtrusive for the viewing visitors. It consisted of a long five-track sector table pivoting at the far end where there was a loco-length traverser. At the Aylesbury end the sector table could be lined up to the single line to Aylesbury or two short spurs for storing locos or brake vans. Later the far two sector tracks could alternatively be lined up to two long sidings behind the main scenic baseboards for storage of trains. This became necessary for storage as Geoff added more stock, in particular long excursion trains. The sector table was lined up to the appropriate track using a simple bolt and this also fed track current to the sector table to prevent stored trains being accidentally driven off any unaligned track with the resultant drop of four feet to the hard floor below. The front of the five sector tracks was split into five electrical sections worked by push buttons for storage of locos. All the track in the fiddle yard was lightly pinned onto cork to reduce noise. The sector and traverser were worked using old Meccano gears and chains, a product that had delighted Geoff in his childhood, and a small control panel was installed behind the fiddle yard board.

THE GAS WORKS

The prototypical curve into the 1889 station provided a triangular area in the loft behind the station and this allowed for the gradual addition of several 'mini baseboards' (or modules) carrying scenery to build up a realistic Aylesbury background. The largest of these was for the gas works situated right next to the station. With Geoff's work experience with Eastern Gas this was to be a very detailed part of the model and the main gas holder was modelled much larger than most modellers would attempt as he knew how dominating it should be. Again he used an unconventional construction method using circles of hardboard with holes in the centre on a central vertical length of studding separated by locking nuts. The holder cladding itself was added with Plastikard sheet with separate Plastikard sheets for the steel plates added over the top. Various other structures like the retort house were added using Geoff's work experience. One weakness of all the added baseboards was that many are quite small and since removal from the loft it has proved very time consuming to erect the model completely and the location of some smaller parts now remain a mystery. This is one reason why the Risborough and District Model Railway Club have only exhibited the complete model on a few occasions.

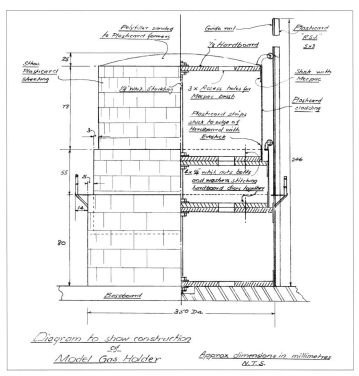

Sketch showing the construction of the main gas holder. The main structure consists of hardboard discs spaced on threaded studding using locking nuts. The outer shell is from Pastikard sheet with separate Plastikard 'plating' over the top.

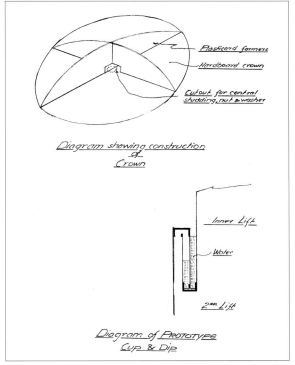

Sketch showing the construction of the gas holder crown with details of the prototype 'cup & dip' gas-seal. Geoff's professional working technical knowledge informed the design and construction of the model.

The gas works

The station showing how the adjacent gas holders dominate the scene just as in real life, but rarely modelled. The open gate in the fence allows a glimpse of the milk dock.

Another gas works building, the purifiers with curved corrugated iron roof, built from Geoff's first-hand experience.

From his professional knowledge Geoff knew how to create a typical gas works atmosphere. The tar tank wagon was a permanent fixture on the model. The building in the centre of the picture is the retort house.

A panoramic view of the gas works yard but also showing the atmosphere of busy activity in the coal yard. Geoff's carefully hand lettered signs and notice boards add to the authentic period atmosphere. A Lesney Aveling & Porter road roller is parked by the gas works wall.

STEAM SHED

Another important feature of the model was the engine shed (steam shed in LNWR parlance) which had to span three baseboards. In LMS days the prototype shed had been shortened so to produce a correct pre-group scene this was quite a long model. He used Plastikard for the construction which was quite thick to add rigidity. The finished model was bedded onto the model using just Polyfilla so that although the whole layout was permanently built into the loft the engine shed could be removed fairly easily if required with the loss of just some replaceable Polyfilla. This was to pay off when the model was eventually removed from the loft as the shed was successfully removed from the layout with no damage. The same principle was used with the footbridge model, described later, with similar success.

Alongside the steam shed, modified GEM George the Fifth kit, No. 2495 *Bassethound,* with scratch-built brass chassis and K's tender unit powering the tender.

Photo P. J. Kelley c. 1971

A rare early colour view across the layout with Whale Experiment No. 828 *City of Liverpool* on shed.

CONTROL PANEL

Another feature of the layout of which Geoff was very proud was the main control panel. This was designed so that the traction current was fed through section switches for about seven main circuits (remember this was decades before DCC!) with seven dead-ends being controlled using push buttons which allowed them to be used for storing a locomotive. There was also a lever frame for all the points and signals using over twenty levers and these were interlocked by a series of hand turned tufnol bobbins with copper at one end fixed to the levers and sliding between phosphor bronze contacts. This meant that a train could not be signalled until the correct points were turned and once signalled the points could not be altered. He never attempted to link the traction current to the points and signals reasoning that if an engine driver wanted to go mad he could! The power was initially through an H&M unit but after some impressive demonstrations at the Easter MRC shows he bought a Codar with its famous inertia effect and paddle braking. This was a very successful change. Later still 'cab-control' was installed for use when a train was run from one end to the other although normally the main layout and the fiddle yard were worked independently.

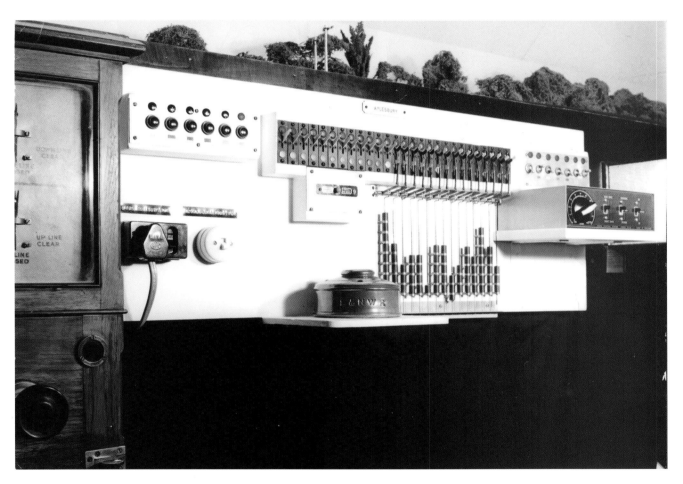

The Aylesbury control panel complete with Codar power supply on the right. The seven section switches above the Codar operated the main track sections of the model, e.g. passenger reception, goods reception, part of the loco shed, etc. while the push buttons on the left worked six siding ends that could be used to isolate and store a locomotive. The levers, by H&M, all worked either points or signals and the sliding tufnol and copper bobbins gave a locking facility between points and signals by sliding between phosphor bronze contacts. There was no locking to traction current. *Photo P. J. Kelley c.1971*

A NEW WORKSHOP

Having discovered the benefit of a separate workshop at Cheshunt, Geoff modified a redundant brick-built coal bunker, once the heating system was changed to a gas-fired variety, into a cosy workshop at Cuffley which was accessible from the house without going out in the weather. This was fitted out with his beloved Unimat lathe, a pillar drill and various other tools. The dining room at Cuffley was also an ideal place for modelling. It was near the family yet with very low slate window sills and a beautiful garden to see outside it provided a good atmosphere for concentrated modelling. It was often easier to move his tray of tools onto the dining table than make the effort to go to the workshop. He was comfortable there, sometimes a bit too much so, on one occasion burning a hole in the table cover with a soldering iron and sometimes burning holes in his clothes. One advantage of working in the house was that there was always someone on hand to help search for any tiny part that might be dropped onto the floor – and a plain carpet was an easier place to search than the box of scrap metal beneath the bench in the workshop!

With his engineering background Geoff always strove to make a 'good mechanical job' of anything he made, be it connected to model railways or anything else. His visits to those Easter exhibitions triggered many long friendships with people who he respected and from whom he learnt a lot. These included Geoff Platt, a well known LNWR expert but also an accomplished modeller. An even greater influence was J. P. (Jim) Richards who was ten years his senior and coincidentally exactly fifty years older than Geoff's son Pete. Jim would suggest construction ideas, sometimes sending sample pieces of his own. Geoff first met Jim at the MRC show when he exhibited his model of an LNWR meat van and Jim questioned the colour it was painted. The friendship and letters continued for the rest of his life. Sometimes Geoff would spend a weekend with Jim at his home near Dolgellau in Wales, sometimes on his own and sometimes with other members of the family. Jim stayed with the family at Cuffley on at least two occasions.

Geoff with long time friend J.P. (Jim) Richards (1903-1999), at Jim's home in Chirk in 1992.
Mike Williams

Diagram 45 meat van scratchbuilt from shellac-coated card in the 1950s and originally, incorrectly, painted white. It was this model that introduced Geoff to J. P. (Jim) Richards who noted the incorrect livery when it was exhibited at the MRC Easter show at Central Hall Westminster and was Geoff's only model ever to be repainted.

The other end of the ballast train of mainly Ratio plastic wagon kits with a modified D&S white metal Diagram 16 10-ton brake van converted for ballast use with an open veranda, the boarding of which was painted red. Much research went into creating this model.

LOCOMOTIVES FOR AYLESBURY

Eventually there were to be about fifteen locos to run on Aylesbury, all but one being built by Geoff. The odd one out was a well-built but sparsely detailed model of an LNWR 4-6-0 19in goods that Geoff had often admired at the Easter MRC show it London. It had been built in the early 1950s by well-known modeller Arthur Hancox and was owned by his friend Bill Michel by the time Geoff first saw it and for some years Geoff would say to Bill 'if you ever want to sell that engine please let me know'. After a few years Bill's health started to deteriorate and he offered it to Geoff for what he had paid for it. It was the only loco on the layout that was unlined and Geoff left it that way although it was converted to EM.

19in Goods No. 2508 built in the early 1950s by Arthur Hancox and converted to EM gauge for Aylesbury.

Francis Webb of Crewe created this famous locomotive which soon earned the nickname "Jumbo". . An indication of its powerful performances.

L.N.W.R. "Precedent" class 2-4-0 Locomotive.
Our kit is all metal and complete with chassis, wheels, coupling rods, etc. XT60 Motor is an extra. Name and number plates are available at 8/10 per set.

Price . . . £7 0s. 6d.
XT60 Motor . 15s. 6d.

GEM 1968 CATALOGUE is now available. Send for your copy.
2/6 post free.

If you have any difficulty in obtaining GEM products locally please order direct from us. We offer prompt and efficient " by return " attention to your orders.

George E. Mellor <small>GEM</small> QUALITY PRODUCTS IN OO and TT GAUGES
31A RHOS ROAD, RHOS-ON-SEA, COLWYN BAY, NORTH WALES

Geoff could not resist some of the LNWR cast whitemetal loco kits produced by George E. Mellor (GEM) and advertised in the model railway press in the 1960s.

Based on a GEM 'Jumbo' kit, Precedent No. 860 *Merrie Carlisle* incorporated much added detail including the rivets but was powered by the Triang XT60 motor as recommended in the kit. *Mike Williams 1989*

In the 1950s and early 1960s there were few LNWR loco kits on the market apart from the K's Coal Tank, hence his scratchbuilt models, but soon GEM Kits (George E. Mellor) appeared on the scene with a succession of LNWR kits which Geoff could not resist. He would usually build his own chassis and he always checked models for accuracy before putting kits together. Many GEM models were added to the stud over the years including a Jumbo 2-4-0 (with scratchbuilt nickel silver splashers as the kit ones didn't line up with the wheels!), a 2-4-2 4ft 6in tank (which he cut in half horizontally to lower it to the correct height and proportions), a 4-6-0 Experiment (which he cut in half vertically to alter it to scale length for his scratchbuilt chassis instead of the intended Triang B12) and a 4-4-0 George the Fifth (in which he fitted a K's tender drive unit so he could add cab details). The GEM 0-6-2 Watford tank was built as intended although still with a scratchbuilt chassis! All these models were highly detailed with added rivet detail (GEM kits never had rivets) except the George the Fifth and some even had dummy inside motion. Adding the Plastikard rivets was the suggestion of youngest son Mike and it was he who added them to the models. A Millholme 4-6-2 tank kit was another favourite and similarly detailed. He usually used K's motors but both the 4-6-2 tank and the Experiment were fitted with Portescap motors and gave impressive performance.

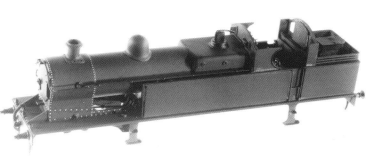

4-6-2 Superheater Tank model during construction from a Millholme kit, showing the numerous Plastikard rivets added before final painting as the kit had no rivets.

Geoff's first scratch built loco, LNWR 2-4-0 Chopper Tank No. 2240 was built in the late-1950s. Geoff was inspired to build this model after seeing Ross Pochin's 7mm version at the Easter Show in the 1950s. Ross supplied Geoff with drawings and photographs. Geoff also corresponded with Stan Garlick who also built a Chopper Tank in S scale, described in *Model Railway News* in December 1962. Built before Geoff had a proper workshop or lathe, the turned parts were made using files and a Wolf electric drill held against the workbench. Geoff painted and lined the model himself. Wheels were early K's brass, and the motor and flywheel were also by K's.

Completed 4-6-2 Superheater Tank model. This model had a Portescap motor and much added detail including partial dummy valve gear shown here.

The K's 0-6-2 Coal Tank kit was launched in 1958.

Geoff's second Coal Tank No. 252, also built from a K's kit but this time with finescale 'Manchester wheels' and a scratchbuilt chassis with a K's motor and flywheel and brake gear. This one was a particularly slow, smooth runner and was probably built in the late-1960s. *Barry Norman for MRJ in 1989*

Several of the larger GEM kits had tempted Geoff away from his aim to build models suitable for his Aylesbury branch line model, no doubt awakening childhood memories of Euston, and these temptations later spread to carriages too which represented periods way outside his originally intended 1910 period for the model. Scratch-built locos were not forgotten and starting in about 1962 he built a 4-4-2 Precursor tank. This was a favourite prototype for both Geoff and son Bob and he always said it was a jointly-made model. In reality Bob made most of the riveted sheet metal parts but the assembly and chassis were entirely Geoff's work. This model was extremely heavy and was fitted with rare brass driving wheels made by Bond's and it ran beautifully. It was painted and lined by him as usual but he could not face lettering it 'L & N W R' on the tank sides (no PC transfers in those days) so he found some 'L N E R' letters the right size, altered the shading and changed the 'E' to a 'W'.

Excursion trains gave an opportunity to run locomotives and stock not normally seen at Aylesbury. Looking towards Cheddington with an excursion train approaching. Note the allotments beside the line and the fiddle yard just visible in the distance.

Right: Whale Precursor Tank No 528, built in nickel silver with a brass chassis, Bond's brass driving wheels and home-made leading and trailing wheels all turned to 'Manchester standard'. This was a very heavy model but a particularly smooth runner.

Below: Scratchbuilt Precursor Tank No. 528.
Barry Norman for MRJ 1989

Another 'scratchbuilt' loco was a 2-4-0 Samson. This was a must after learning that No 263, *Pheasant* had been the Aylesbury branch engine in the early 1890s. With no kit available for this early locomotive (introduced in 1863), and quite a complex design, scratchbuilding seemed the only thing to do. The curvy footplate still presented a challenge so Bob started drawing up artwork to have these components etched but this soon led to etchings for the whole engine, although the tender was the K's Problem kit which the then owners of K's kits had produced specially. Power was from the then-favoured Portescap but to allow for full cab fittings and fairly high axles (6ft 3in driving wheels) new side frames were produced to replace the Portescap version so the motor could be located to drive the front axle, although this no doubt invalidated the Portescap guarantee. This was the test etch and the alternative gearbox sides were subsequently incorporated in the production etches. He then built a second Samson using the production etch and the result was a beautiful, smooth running model which on this occasion was not painted by Geoff as the family had it painted by Alan Brackenborough as a surprise present for him. This is the kit later added to John Redrup's excellent London Road Models range. Geoff did not build any LRM models only because they came on the market too late for him.

All Geoff's models were well built and in the early-1960s he was very impressed with several features of the Manchester Model Railway Society layout, Presson, and from discussion with Sid Stubbs on that layout he decided to use finescale 'Manchester wheels' on his locos from then on. Sid even gave him a form tool for turning down all loco wheels to these standards in the Unimat lathe although he never attempted to use it on wagon or carriage wheels. For some reason he did not often use Romford wheels although K's were used quite often but from the late-1960s K's wheels were plated with a very hard plating. He had known Ken Keyser of K's for several years and managed to buy some wheels from K's before they went through the plating process so he could turn them to Manchester standards.

The next scratchbuilt loco was Geoff's best and was a Webb 0-6-0 Coal Engine. This was started in the mid-1970s and was very highly detailed with full cab fittings and convincing dummy inside motion. To achieve this detail in the loco he designed his own tender drive with a motor driving the two outer axles and even including a flywheel. The Webb tender design meant the motor had to be mounted fairly low down which caused a problem with the centre axle lifting as it was attracted by the magnet. He overcame this by 'borrowing' one of Beryl's alloy knitting needles. She probably didn't want it back after an inch was cut off it! The model was designed to run very slowly as a goods engine and performed very well although with quite a lot of noise.

Samson class 2-4-0 No. 263 *Pheasant* built from home-made etchings with a K's white metal tender and Portescap motor. It was painted by Alan Brackenborough and is standing in front of Aylesbury locomotive shed.

Scratchbuilt Coal Engine No. 85.   *Mike Williams 1987*

Scratchbuilt Coal Engine No. 85 with tender drive and dummy valve gear.

Experiment 4-6-0 No. 828 *City of Liverpool*. Built from a modified GEM kit with plastikard rivets and a scratchbuilt chassis with Portescap motor. No known connection to Aylesbury but an irresistible prototype.

2-4-2 5ft 6in Tank No. 910 – Scratchbuilt by Geoff in the late-1950s seen here running at Railex in May 2016.

LNWR locomotives running on Aylesbury EM

1. **2-4-0 Chopper Tank No. 2240** – Scratchbuilt in the mid-1950s with a K's motor and flywheel and bought in wheels and buffers. Prototype not known to have run on the Aylesbury Branch, although No. 2234 of the same class is recorded.

2. **2-4-2 5ft 6in Tank No. 910** – Scratchbuilt in late-1950s with K's motor and flywheel. The loco proved to be a little underpowered, limited to three K's six-wheelers and a van. To reduce friction Geoff made a new split-axle insulated chassis *c.*1960, with the front axle and front section of the frames running as a separate pony truck pivoted about the centre of the coupled wheelbase. A larger K's motor and flywheel increased the power. Leading and trailing wheels were improved with the correct number of spokes. The first of the class and the engine to run the last passenger train in 1953 as BR No. 46601, brought back as it had run on the branch in LNWR days when it was numbered 910.

3. **0-6-2 coal tank No. 252** – K's kit with scratchbuilt chassis and first use of turned 'Manchester standard' wheels and added body detail. K's motor and flywheel. Number chosen to suit photos but no known connection to Aylesbury. A previous Coal Tank from a K's kit was run on Aylesbury Mark 1 and was sold with the layout.

4. **2-4-0 improved Precedent No. 860** *Merrie Carlisle* – GEM kit with the recommended Triang XT60 motor with no flywheel but with added detail and scratchbuilt splashers for better alignment with the driving wheels.

5. **2-4-2 4ft 6in Tank No. 1184** – GEM kit with scratchbuilt chassis and added detail. The side tanks and bunker were too high on the kit so, after assembly, it was cut in half horizontally and reduced in height. No. 1184 had no known connections with Aylesbury but was chosen to match some very clear prototype photos used for detailing and hence modelled in earlier pre-coalrails condition.

6. **0-6-2 Watford Tank No. 1593** – GEM kit with scratchbuilt chassis with DS10 motor and much added detail including added Plastikard rivets. Also modelled without coalrails to match clear photos used for detailing but No. 1593 had no known connection to Aylesbury.

7. **4-4-2 Precursor Tank No. 528** – all scratchbuilt, very heavy model with Bonds brass driving wheels and home made bogie and trailing wheels from Nucro centres. No. 528 was the first of the class and chosen to match clear photos. It is unlikely this engine ever went to Aylesbury due to axle loading restrictions.

8. **4-6-2 Superheater Tank No. 962** – Millholme kit with scratchbuilt chassis incorporating a Portescap motor and with much added detail. No. 962 had no known connection to Aylesbury.

9. **4-6-0 19in Goods No. 2508** – scratchbuilt to 16.5mm gauge by Arthur Hancox in the 1950s and bought from Bill Michel and later converted to EM. A nice solid model with sparse detail and the only unlined model on the layout.

10. **4-6-0 Experiment No. 828** *City of Liverpool* – GEM kit with scratchbuilt chassis incorporating a Portescap motor and much added detail including Plastikard rivets. The kit was designed to fit the Triang B12 chassis which had a longer coupled wheelbase so, after assembly, it was cut in half vertically and reduced to scale length. No. 828 had no known connection to Aylesbury.

11. **4-4-0 George the Fifth No. 2495** *Bassethound* – GEM kit with scratchbuilt chassis and added detail. A K's motorised tender drive unit was fitted in the tender to allow full cab details to be fitted. No known connection to Aylesbury.

12. **2-4-0 Samson No. 263** *Pheasant* – known to have been the branch engine in the 1890s, this model was scratchbuilt from home-produced etches, later incorporated in the London Road Models range, with a K's whitemetal tender. The etches included alternative gearbox sideframes to allow a small Portescap motor to be fitted and full cab details as well as dummy inside motion. The only model painted by Alan Brackenborough.

13. **0-6-0 Coal Engine No. 85** – scratchbuilt with home made tender drive driving on outer two axles and incorporating a flywheel. A very detailed model with full cab details and dummy inside motion which ran very slowly and smoothly but was noisy. No. 85 chosen to match clear official photos.

Several other engines were in progress including a Whale Precursor (Brassmasters), Webb Dreadnought compound (M&L) and a Special Tank (modified GEM kit), some of which were almost complete.

COUPLINGS

Another feature of Presson which Geoff admired was the Alex Jackson coupling and he did experiments with two suitably equipped test vehicles, although in the end he continued with the couplings he already had. This was partly due to the large amount of stock (even then) that he would have to convert but he also felt it needed very accurate construction and he wasn't convinced of its ability to work on some of the reverse curves and gradients on parts of the layout.

Couplings on the model were non-standard too. Geoff wanted couplings that could be uncoupled automatically by magnet beneath the baseboard. The couplings he chose were Rivarossi which although quite obtrusive, avoiding the dreaded wire across the buffers, were reliable and at the time were easily obtainable. However, to retain at least one 'photographic' end of all vehicles he fitted his own simple wire hook at one end with the Rivarossi at the other. When completing a model, he chose which was its best side concerning detail, painting, lining, lettering, etc and then fitted the coupling to show the best side. Remember that with the permanent installation in the loft only one side could be seen, although he did always fully finish both.

That was not quite the end of the story of couplings at Aylesbury though as Rivarossi stopped making 'his' couplings. With so much stock already running he therefore developed his own smaller, neater version, made in a jig he built for all future construction. These worked just like the Rivarossi including the magnetic uncoupling facility and he christened them 'Aylesbury couplings'.

CARRIAGES AND WAGONS

Another influence was Gordon Hayward who used to demonstrate lettering 7mm scale private owner wagons at the Easter shows – Geoff never used transfers to letter his PO wagons. Despite building many appropriate private owner wagons these were all relevant to the post group period as he was unable to find details of suitable pre-group wagons. He reasoned that although these were out of period at least they did relate to Aylesbury. Some of these were lettered on old Trackmaster plastic bodies, some were Peco but others were scratchbuilt, often on Peco underframes. Just one wagon was inappropriate to Aylesbury and that was 'Tottenham District Light Heat and Power Company' which he built as a reminder of his days starting work with Eastern Gas in north London.

Although he built several engines he also loved building carriages and wagons. At first these were carefully selected to be suitable for running to Aylesbury and to do that he would use kits if they were available (but always modified or corrected where he felt it necessary) or built from scratch. His favourite material for carriage sides and ends was etched zinc and he had some of the earliest etches produced by Trevor Charlton of Sutton Coldfield and eventually quite a lot of the stock was etched zinc. Later, especially when his health stopped him going into the loft to see the railway, he made anything that took his fancy, ranging from an 1850s carriage (modelled from measurements taken from a grounded body found in Northamptonshire) to a twelve-wheeled dining saloon and even a conversion of two six-wheeled carriages onto a bogie underframe finished in LMS livery.

Geoff accepted that wagons from other railway companies would at times find their way to Aylesbury and built several non-LNWR wagons but always from kits, preferring to spend scratchbuilding time on LNWR stock. However, even then each model was properly researched and modifications made to kits where he felt they were warranted and of course the correct livery was always applied by hand. There was a lot of cattle and horse traffic at Aylesbury and several models of non-LNWR horse boxes and cattle wagons were built to provide more realistic special trains.

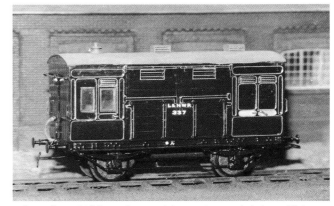

One of two 21ft horse box models running on Aylesbury. This one was made using Trevor Charlton etched zinc sides and ends which was Geoff's preferred material for carriage stock and seemed to take paint better than etched brass.

Micro Rail kit for a 14ft 6in horse box.   *Mike Williams 1988*

42ft seven-compartment third class radial carriage built from some of the very earliest Trevor Charlton etched zinc sides and ends with a partially etched brass underframe.

50ft corridor brake third modelled on a conversion by the LNWR just before the grouping. The model was based on a Ratio plastic kit but with the van end replaced with parts from Roxey Mouldings.

The end of a Euston-Rugby set of 50ft lavatory stock running as an excursion to Aylesbury. The models were built using Trevor Charlton etched zinc sides and ends on a modified Ratio underframe.

Geoff loved building stock of all kinds and this view includes some scratchbuilt and some kit-built models. The SE&CR van was a cast white metal kit, the NLR open wagon a modified Ratio plastic kit and the roof-door vans cast white metal D&S kits. The two private owner wagons both had scratchbuilt Plastikard bodies and were hand-painted to match identified wagons running to Aylesbury after the grouping.

Here is Geoff's first scratchbuilt loco, Chopper Tank No. 2240 heading a ballast train consisting of mainly Ratio plastic wagon kits and a K's white metal all third 30ft 1in carriage as modified to a riding van. Note some of the doors lack door handles representing doors that had been screwed-up closed.

Apart from the many Aylesbury-related PO wagons, all hand lettered, this photo shows the scratchbuilt 'Boff' van, identified by Jim Richards from a pre-group photograph, taken at Aylesbury. It is standing in the siding at the end of the platform being loaded with milk churns from a mainly scratchbuilt lorry built to photographs of Nestlé lorries from the pre-group period. Note the timber earth-filled buffer stop, typical of the stops at Aylesbury at the time.

This love of building rolling stock eventually led to operational problems as he always worried about damage caused by handling. For that reason, once a model was completed and placed on the layout it was never taken off again, leading to severe congestion on what should have been a sleepy branch line terminus. He had at least two excursion trains of main line stock which therefore had to be accommodated on the layout and it was these that really led to the construction of the two long sidings behind the long scenic baseboard. The original aim to run to a scale actual timetable was therefore rarely achievable although this was probably not noticed by most of the visitors who mostly wanted to admire and talk.

Although Geoff lined all his LNWR locos by hand almost all the carriages were lined by his son, Bob. Carriages are much easier to line than locomotives as the lining just follows the beading and his locos proved he could certainly line by hand – he never used lining transfers – and he may have been happy for Bob to line the carriages as he enjoyed the feeling of sharing his hobby with the family. Youngest son, Mike, who was born in 1957 also followed his father's interest in railways, again mainly LNWR, but in 7mm finescale and Geoff enjoyed encouraging Mike too, suggesting a small baseboard in the loft to display Mike's beautiful models. Mike later moved up to Gauge 3 and set up the model manufacturing business of Williams Models.

PERSPECTIVE MODELLING

Perhaps the feature of Geoff's model of Aylesbury that made it famous, apart from the fact that it was, unusually for the 1960s, a model of a real station, was his use of perspective modelling. He had a rule that any railway buildings were built to 4mm scale but he also wanted to create the effect of Aylesbury outside the railway boundary. This presented thought provoking problems in a few areas especially as there were two roads, High Street and Park Street over the level crossing, which were at right angles to the front of the baseboard.

Park Street in particular was a problem because the prototype road continued up to a T-junction and his model was less than 18in wide at that point. Geoff's answer was to gently slope the road up to the desired height by the back scene, at the same time reducing its width. The rows of houses either side also had to follow the road of course but finish up at the correct height on the back scene to create the correct distance effect. To achieve this, he made plain crude cardboard buildings with only the vertical lines being parallel. These were stuck together with Sellotape, put in place on the model and then viewed from the set viewing position. Adjustments were made using scissors and more Sellotape until Geoff, and the family (!), agreed the effect was right. The buildings were then dismantled and used as templates to make proper models from Plastikard. The effect was enhanced by using a reducing scale

Park Street level crossing from the optimum viewing position, disguising the total baseboard width of just 2ft. So many features make this recognisable to those who knew the line including the signalmen's cottages, level crossing, footbridge, signal box, signal, Norfolk Terrace and many other features.
Photograph by Andy York, BRM magazine

Looking down on Park Street giving some idea of the foreshortening of the scenery. This view was taken *c.*1971, before the footbridge was added. Note how the nearest siding stops short of the crossing, allowing room for the boarded cart track into the basket works to be accurately modelled. Two styles of buffer stop are shown.

A busy view of Park Street level crossing with a ballast train trundling past.

Looking across the layout to Norfolk Terrace with two platelayers busy working outside their hut. *Mike Williams 1989*

Ganger's trolley and grindstone by the PW hut.

A general view of Aylesbury Mark 1 taken from where the footbridge would have been but was never built. The large goods yard was not modelled at all and the track layout simplified in some areas. Note the single slip just the other side of the crossing was not modelled but just the catch point that Geoff had seen himself. Later research also revealed other inaccuracies like the short loco shed, the lack of a toilet on the signal box landing and the passenger run round buffer stop on the left did not stop short for the cart track into the basket works.

Norfolk Terrace built following photographs and help from several residents. The platelayers seem to be busy outside their hut. The LNWR runner wagon would not have been used at Aylesbury but was fitted with a 'push-only' coupling at the left hand end to aid shunting in inaccessible areas.

for features like people so that a 2mm scale man crossing the road in Park Street was positioned the correct distance back to match the building height at that point.

Two other significant buildings around Park Street level crossing were the signalmen's cottages and the signal box. The cottages were built from Ballard embossed card as had been used on the station building and care was taken to include all the details Geoff was able to see on the real thing including number plates affixed to the walls and garden sheds. The signal box was a standard LNWR design but still needed detailed research to represent the true LNWR period look. The final structure near Park Street was Norfolk Terrace which went along the backscene of the model and was made in Plastikard. This was light, as it was to be detachable, but carefully braced to avoid warping. The model was slightly smaller than 4mm scale to create the distance illusion and was carefully coloured to create the right effect.

Aylesbury signal box, with the point rodding and footbridge still to be added *c*.1971.   *P. J. Kelley*

HIGH STREET

High Street, across the frontage of the station, was more complicated because it starts off being viewed across the road from the station but as it goes back across the baseboard the perspective modelling has to start and the buildings begin to taper. The same principles were used as had been used in Park Street but this led to some complicated, odd-shaped buildings. The Chandos Hotel almost opposite the station was a tricky building to get right because not only did it need the perspective effect but it was a more complex structure and even included balconies with iron railings. The distance across to the goods yard was also made to look longer as non-railway buildings became smaller and smaller. All the perspective scenery was built assuming a normal viewing height of a few inches above the baseboards. Geoff knew, and corresponded with, Jack Nelson for many years and some of these ideas may have come from him.

View along High Street showing the perspective modelling of the buildings.

THE PRISON

At the other extreme, Aylesbury prison is a prominent feature beside the line on the Cheddington side of Park Street. It is a large, complex brick structure which Geoff did not have the enthusiasm to construct in detail as it was a non-railway building. His answer was to stand on the track and take a photograph of it. He then worked out how wide it needed to be printed to give the correct distance effect on the model and the local photographer produced a print to the right length. All he then had to do was give it a brick red water colour wash – or so he thought! Geoff then realised that the building had a lot of white stone detailing which he then had to add back by hand so it still turned into a long job in the end.

Geoff's first scratchbuilt locomotive, 2-4-0T Chopper Tank No. 2240 posed in front of Aylesbury prison *c*.1971. The prison was an enlargement of a photograph taken by Geoff and reproduced to the length required to give the right distance effect. Note all the white stone highlighting on the building that had to be applied separately to the photograph after it had been colour-washed. *P. J. Kelley*

The prison, as seen at Railex in May 2016. The baseboard is 2ft wide at this point but the illusion of much greater distance is achieved. Note the allotments alongside the railway, planted with cabbages made from cloves. *Photograph by Andy York, BRM magazine*

BACKSCENE

The prison was one of the longest items on the backscene but of course backscene was needed for the entire length of the model in one form or another. This was a mixture of semi-relief, whole buildings or just painted on the back board, the format being chosen as appropriate. To retain the important perspective most of this was to less than 4mm scale, diminishing with distance from the viewing position. Although Geoff did much research into the Aylesbury features that were to be represented there were other, unexpected, complications. From the normal viewing position when the viewer scanned the background the curve meant that the length of apparent backscene was longer than the railway model in the foreground. This, coupled with the backscene being to a smaller scale, meant that, even including all the features that had been researched, it was 'not long enough' for the model. Here some artistic licence was taken and several strategically placed trees helped to space the backscene features so that they all appeared in the right place to the viewer. Some of the backscene was only visible between railway or gas works features and this forced the viewer to see some features from a fixed viewpoint which helped partially to overcome this problem.

Part of the backscene glimpsed between the two gas holders. This was Railway Street, so named as it led to the first, 1839, passenger station. All these buildings were modelled to less than 4mm scale and diminishing in size to create the backscene illusion.

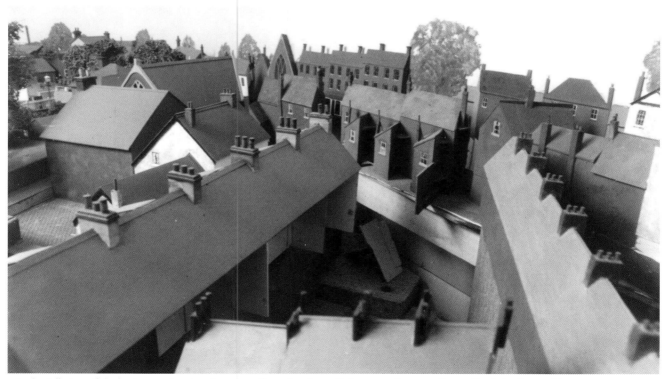

An 'aerial' view of the backscene showing the secret of creating the realistic scene when seen from a fixed viewing position.

Another 'bird's eye' view of part of the backscene. Details were only modelled if they could be seen from the fixed viewing position.

Part of the nearer backscene made by reference to photographs, some of which was transferred from the photograph using a squared grid. The buildings behind the fence are modelled in low-relief.

Further painted backscene behind the goods yard from photographs and observation.

Left: Another view of Railway Street. The black building is the timber-built goods shed. The cattle wagon is parked on the track which was the original 1839 platform line.

A general view of the backscene showing the mix of scales, complete buildings (Norfolk Terrace on the right), low relief (oil depot) and painted features.

LATERAL THINKING

Geoff often indulged in lateral thinking in his modelling and there are several examples on Aylesbury. Much of the grass on the model was along the front of the baseboard and because of its height (about 55in above the floor as it rested on top of the roof timbers in the loft) he knew that some visitors would hold onto the edge and so the grass was made of some textured Polyfilla painted green so that it could be easily repaired. This remained one of the least convincing parts of the model. For the same reason some of the iron railings near the front were made from plastic hair combs bought from Woolworths with just a cotton run along just down from the top. He often spoke about telling the assistant in Woolworths why he wanted two dozen combs that had to be the same colour! Eventually etched iron railings became available and he did replace some of these for example around the Park Street level crossing. There are quite a few allotments on the model too and these include cloves as cabbages, painted two shades of green. These actually look very effective and provoke many comments, but nobody notices that they are probably a scale one and a half feet across! This is another of Geoff's illusions. The row of mature trees lining the track on the north side going eastwards from the Park Street level crossing were another challenge where the family helped as they were made using twisted wire, Beryl's hair and tea-leaves sprayed green with brown trunks. The model trees available at the time were too small for those required on the model at this location.

THE FOOTBRIDGE

One of the most detailed features on the model is probably the footbridge. This was a typical LNWR design incorporating a wheel casting in the balustrade for every step. After thinking about this for years Colin Waite – who made etched wagon underframe units – offered to help and, following Geoff producing the artwork, a set of parts were etched which Geoff then soldered together. This was quite advanced in the 1970s as few people were etching right through at that time but it remains a fine model over forty years later and is to be added to the LRM range eventually. Like the loco shed, this too straddled more than one baseboard and so was built on a solid base and bedded on Polyfilla for easy removal when required in the future. This forward thinking saved the model from damage when the layout was eventually dismantled.

Right: The footbridge looking towards the station. For years the footbridge was missing from the layout while Geoff worked out a way to model it realistically. Fortunately Geoff had the foresight to measure and photograph the prototype before it was demolished in the 1960s and this information was later used to design a set of custom etches.
Photograph by Andy York, BRM magazine

Precedent No. 860 *Merrie Carlisle* departs for Cheddington under the footbridge, Railex 2016.   *Photograph by Andy York, BRM magazine*

A general view of Aylesbury footbridge, missing from the layout for so long while Geoff worked out how to build a model of such an intricate design. It was an early use of brass etching using etching right through (i.e. from both sides) rather than half-etched and was developed with much help from Colin Waite. Geoff had some official drawings and drew his own artwork and made his own column patterns for casting.

The etched footbridge model.   *Mike Williams 1989*

A very enlarged view of some of the etched footbridge detail, showing the landing lattice work and X-bracing.

More enlarged detail of the etched footbridge. The distinctive wheel-pattern cast balustrades were an LNWR standard style.

SIGNALS

Some of the last parts of the model to be built were the signals although the levers and interlocking were built into the control panel from the start. The Ratio LNWR signals were not then available so, after some false starts at scratch-building, all the semaphore signals Geoff made used white metal components cast by K's for Jack Nelson to 3.5mm to the foot scale. The arms were vulnerable being whitemetal but the signals were solidly mounted through the baseboard in copper tubing with point motors mounted at the bottom. All lamps, guy wires, etc. were added as appropriate. Jack Nelson didn't make ground signals so these were scratchbuilt in brass. All signals were working so that the ground signals rotated through ninety degrees as per the prototype.

The footbridge completes the scene in this view towards Cheddington with the ballast train awaiting instruction. Some of the earlier plastic comb iron railings have been replaced with more delicate etched brass.

Park Street level crossing with a coal train about to depart behind Coal Engine No. 85. All wagons were hand lettered. The 'Tottenham District Light, Heat & Power Co.' wagon was not appropriate for Aylesbury but was painted by Geoff as a reminder of the early days of his career with Eastern Gas. *Mike Williams 1989*

A general view of the approach to the station, gas works and goods yard from near rail level. Note the smooth track alignment.

A view from the gas works showing the spacious effect of the model. The excursion train approaching the station consists of PC Models corridor stock and is hauled by George the Fifth No. 2495 *Bassethound*.
P. J. Kelley c.1971

General view of the line looking towards Cheddington with the line of chestnut trees, with just one poplar as per the real thing. Note the use of black plastic hair combs to represent iron railings. Asked by the shop assistants why he needed eighteen identical black plastic combs Geoff replied he was making a fence around the allotment … but they had both disappeared.

Occupation crossing at the end of the long goods headshunt. The medium cattle wagon with lime-washed lower sides is scratchbuilt.

A general view of the line on the Cheddington side of Park Street with the ballast train *c.*1984.

A passenger train to Cheddington just past Park Street. Note the home made trees on the right and the extensive allotments on the left. The locomotive is 5ft 6in Tank No. 910.

Eventually the model was finished although there were two features that were never completed. One of these was a small ground frame that should have been fitted at the end of the siding finishing in front of the prison. The other was the uncoupling magnets which were never fitted beneath the baseboards, so that the 'automatic' couplings so carefully created over the years were always worked by using a piece of hand-held wire. This was generally acceptable but did cause difficulties operationally when uncoupling was required under the station screen or in the goods yard over the wide baseboards at that point. The latter was partially overcome by shunting using a model of an LNWR runner wagon (that would never have been used at Aylesbury) with a coupling at one end that could only be used to push and would not actually couple up.

Gradually Aylesbury Mark Two became more well known with groups of model railway enthusiasts often meeting at the house in Cuffley to see the model and also to enjoy a railway chat downstairs. Soon a group of like-minded modellers was formed which called themselves 5516 (the number of Patriot class *The Bedfordshire and Hertfordshire Regiment*) as most of the 'members' lived in those two counties. Meetings were held at the houses of various members of the group. Many other groups met at the house over a period of about thirty-five years with often up to twenty at a time taking turns to go in the loft to see the model so that only about five at a time were in the

loft. The restriction was to limit weight due to a removed roof truss although Geoff felt his triangulation was a strong enough replacement.

It must be recorded that Geoff's wife Beryl was remarkably supportive at these meetings which were attended almost entirely by men and she supplied tea, coffee and sometimes snacks or sandwiches where appropriate. Not only was this a considerable amount of hard work but it was usually done on her own as few visitors took the time to discuss non-railway matters downstairs, although some did venture into the garden with her to talk about plants. Geoff's biggest regret when looking back from the mid-1990s was that he never kept a visitors' book but it is known that the number of visitors over those thirty-five years was well into three figures, several guests visiting many times and some even making unplanned stays overnight! Geoff made many good friends through these meetings and several showed their appreciation by not only bringing gifts for Beryl but sometimes models for Geoff. Mike Peascod gave him a very detailed scratchbuilt carriage to run as a special through carriage while others like Dave Lowery brought a nicely weathered wagon. Sometimes visitors would bring a model of their own to run, the most impressive probably being a scratchbuilt LNER Beyer-Garratt.

As the layout became known through the meetings mentioned above and articles in *Model Railway News* and

Geoff enjoyed watching the trains go by more than driving them himself.

Studio Cole Ltd

A general view probably taken *c.*1970 showing considerable areas of scenery still to be built. The prototype station was at a lower level than the goods yard, with a falling gradient towards the buffer stops which enabled shunting and running round of carriages by gravity. Geoff created the illusion of different levels by slightly raising the goods yard behind the engine shed, with a gradient commencing at the points where they branched off the loco shed road.   *Studio Cole Ltd*

Geoff taking in the loft atmosphere in the early 1970s.   *Studio Cole Ltd*

Geoff at the controls of his model in 1989. This shows the model in its loft setting with various relics displayed opposite. Note he proudly wears his LNWR Society tie. He was Society Secretary from 1981-88 and President for several years up to his death in 1998. The fiddle yard can just be seen at the far end.   *Mike Williams*

Geoff watching the trains go by in 1989. He grew a beard from the day he retired in Spring 1974.
Mike Williams

Model Railway Journal Geoff started to be invited to give talks on the branch line and his model. These often took him to different parts of the country, and introduced him to more enthusiasts some of whom subsequently visited the layout at Cuffley.

As the collection of books, photographs, drawings, etc grew so an extension was built along the front of the house. Nicknamed 'the library', this provided more space and interest during meetings. Geoff's modelling table was often found in 'the library' where his latest modelling work-in-progress could be viewed and often visitors would discuss the solution to a constructional problem he had encountered. One example was Brian Rogers, of Ultrascale Wheels, who helped out with chassis design.

Geoff died in October 1998 and eventually Beryl moved and the house was sold. In readiness for this 'Aylesbury' was carefully dismantled and stored by Geoff's son Mike to whom much gratitude is owed for its survival. Some of the baseboards had sections added which made them slightly too wide for the loft trap door so the opening was carefully enlarged and neatly painted. It was not expected at the time that the subsequent owner of the house was going to demolish it!

Aylesbury restored – Tim Peacock

I first became aware of this iconic layout many years ago when it appeared in early editions of *MRJ* and then many years later, there it was again, advertised in the *EMGS Journal* looking for a new home. It transpired that there had been little interest and that it would be disposed of if no one could be found to take it on.

I arranged with Mike Williams (one of the builder's sons) to view the layout and then hired a van and brought it home. For some time, it remained in store in my layout shed while its fate was decided. I am a member of the Risborough and District Model Railway Club and I suggested the club could take it on as a club project. There was sufficient interest, so storage space was cleared and the layout moved to its new abode.

Some time was spent determining what was needed to display the layout and get it running again.

There were three issues:

1. Electrics
When the layout was removed from its original home in the loft, all the wires to the control panel had been cut and labelled. Unfortunately, many of the labels had fallen off and the transformers and other associated mains connections didn't meet modern safety standards. There was a wonderful hand built electro-mechanical interlocking board which would have been nice to restore.

2. Display Stand
There was no means of elevating the layout to the desired viewing height which was important for the forced perspective elements to work properly. The reason for this, quite simply was the layout had previously been built in and onto the roof timbers of the loft.

3. General wear and tear
Over the years and in removing it from the original loft, minor damage had been done to structures and scenery.

Solutions

Electrics. It was decided that trying to reverse engineer all the wiring was a mission too far, so the decision was made to convert the layout to DCC operation. This is one area where the club expertise is strong. All the original wiring was removed except the rail droppers. Several buses were installed and the old droppers connected to these. The original PO relays for point switches were retained and operated using Digitrax DS 64s. One Frog Juicer was used to sort out frog polarities for the combined complex crossing and crossovers in the yard. Meanwhile, the locos were taken away for servicing and conversion to DCC. All were found to still be smooth running and conversion presented no difficulties. The only casualty of this approach was the electro-mechanical interlocking board. However, Bob Williams confided that is was never really reliable, so perhaps that was a blessing in disguise!

Display. The layout is displayed quite high and a system of trestles was constructed from Ikea shelving supports from the Ivar range. This has proved robust, relatively simple to erect and stable (also reasonably cheap!). The biggest problem with the layout is its weight. Constructed on massive boards, it weighs a ton and moving it about is no mean task. To that end, the decision has been taken not to go on the exhibition circuit. The risk of damage to it and us is too great. However, it is intended that it should go on more permanent public display in due course.

Repairs. A team of modellers with the required talents set about making good the various bits of damage. Restoration was sympathetic to the original modelling style (no static grass here) and careful use of colour to blend in with the old. Finally, refurbishment and enhancement of the backscene was commissioned as the old one was a bit low and very tired looking. The new one is sympathetic in style to the original modelling and sets off the model perfectly.

TIM PEACOCK
President of Risborough and District Model Railway Club
(founded 1971)

Restoring the backscene – Paul Bambrick

The restoration of the Aylesbury High Street backscene began with a telephone call from Andrew David of the Risborough & District MRC, who invited me to come and see the layout at their club rooms. The brief was to sympathetically restore Geoff's original hardboard panels, which featured some 3D relief elements as part of the presentation.

3D backscenes were practically unheard of in Geoff's day, and this particular layout was really presented as a diorama. It was such a significant exercise in landscaping and forced perspective that I felt that the restoration of the whole model was definitely worthwhile, so I agreed to undertake the restoration on a voluntary basis.

I arranged for a further visit to record and take photographs, which would then allow me to remove the panels and work on them at home. As I remember they were quite low in height compared to the modern 3D efforts that we see nowadays, and I practically had to bend them into the van as gently as possible so as not to incur any damage. Once they were propped up in the studio, I began the process of researching what Geoff had represented and look at the best way to conserve his existing work.

The panels were redone by firstly working my way round, repairing any damaged and frayed edges of the hardboard with car body filler. With a decent repaired surface to work on and, and a set of joggled joins accurately aligned, I took a swatch of the sky base colour and had a matched pot of paint mixed up.

I could now re-do the sky surface, including a few small patches of cloud here and there, and once the sky was refinished, I could pay attention to reinstating the visible areas of ground surface between buildings. Once I had a distant skyline depicted, the painted 2D trees could be re-instated, because of course you can't represent a tree on a picture without first having done the background.

Geoff's modelling style was extremely effective, but as with so many craftsmen there was a recognisable hand in the way that he represented buildings. He mixed different colour intensities for different facing walls for instance, which is a landscape (or townscape in this case) painting technique to depict the effect of directional light fall. With a layout scale building this isn't done, as the effect happens naturally, so scale modellers never use this method, but as we start to include forced perspective relief buildings, with progressively smaller scales and flatter footprints, a painted lightfall helps to suggest more form to the structures than they actually have. Geoff instinctively understood how to blend from layout scale to distance by combining both modellers and painters techniques.

Getting a panorama presented as accurately as possible involves doing my usual research, and a good part of this process is finding old photographs and studying period mapping to prevent unnecessary guesswork. This was really following in Geoff's footsteps, but in my normal day-to-day backscene work I rely on this reference to produce a landscape with no recognisable style at all. Because this was an exercise in conservation though, I deliberately used the techniques and colours that Geoff chose, rather than any of my own approaches. It is often the case that there is little in the way of detailed work on the buildings and roof lines depicted in a forced perspective diorama, especially towards the middle to far distance, so I made a point of carefully reproducing this language during the whole restoration.

There were a small number of gaps in the rooflines, and some other minor damage like chipped paint and broken and lost chimney stacks, so these, as well as missing windows and doors were replaced and re-instated wherever necessary using Geoff's distinctive style and colour palette to maintain continuity.

At the approach to Aylesbury High Street, the prison wall appears alongside the line as we look to the north west, and beyond that the tower and vicarage of Bierton can be seen in the distance, so this was also repaired and set to distance among trees.

Once the panels were done, they could be aligned and re-fitted, and the best opportunity for this was to spend a few hours on the Friday afternoon before the Railex 2016 exhibition at the Stoke Mandeville stadium, joining in with the other contributors, blending the panels in around the baseboards.

Detail of the backscene showing the tower and spire of St. James the Great church at Bierton with the vicarage alongside.

Railex, Stoke Mandeville 28-29th May 2016

Tim Peacock of the Risborough & District MRC (left) discusses the model with Cliff Parsons. *Photographs Ian Phillips*

By good fortune the Risborough and District Model Railway Club offered the model a home in 2012 and have sympathetically renovated any damaged areas and completely rewired it to current DCC standards. Much of the rolling stock was retained by Geoff's family.

The layout was not originally designed to be exhibited, having been permanently installed in Geoff's loft. Following Geoff's passing the layout was carefully dismantled and stored. The delicate nature of the models and structures make them prone to damage. The layout is made up of many individual baseboards which are time-consuming to align and reassemble. It is worth remembering too that Geoff built the model with the baseboards 55 inches above the floor with the perspective scenery designed to be viewed from this optimum level.

Despite these difficulties, the complete layout was exhibited and run to a realistic timetable at Railex at Stoke Mandeville in May 2016, where very many of those who had seen it at Cuffley and in magazines over the years came to see it again and reminisce with the family including Beryl who also attended on one of the two days.

A selection of magazine articles featuring Geoff Williams' Aylesbury models

Aylesbury Mark 1

Model Railway News	November 1959	'Layout Gallery' LNWR Aylesbury EM gauge
Model Railway News	September 1960	'Layout Gallery' Aylesbury Amended

Aylesbury Mark 2

Model Railway News	January 1964	Editorial note p.164
Model Railway News	May 1964	Aylesbury Altered
Model Railway News	May 1971	Another Aylesbury

The History of Model and Miniature Railways (1974 part-work), p.129.

Model Railway Journal	Issue 0	1985	Aylesbury LNWR
Model Railway Journal	Issue 36	1990	Perspective modelling
Model Railway Journal	Issue 37	1990	The Gas Works
Model Railway Journal	Issue 52	1992	Rolling Stock at Aylesbury
Model Railway Journal	Issue 59	1992	Aylesbury Station

British Railway Modelling	May 2016	Aylesbury LNWR

Model Rail No. 233	April 2017	Aylesbury LNWR

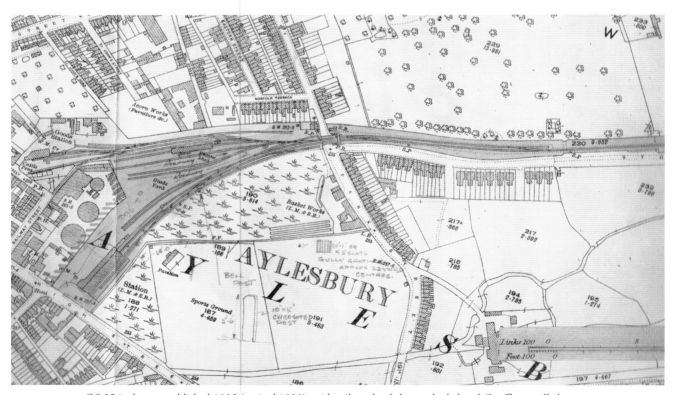

OS 25 inch map published 1925 (revised 1923), with railway land shown shaded and Geoff's pencilled notes.

PART TWO

Researching the Aylesbury Branch

At the time the model was started most model railways were based on imagination with very few representing a real location. This was one of the main aspects of Geoff's model that attracted attention from other modellers and the model press. Researching the entire branch line from Cheddington to Aylesbury became a separate hobby in its own right and in Part Two we explore how Geoff went about it, recording and researching the prototype, and the lengths he went to in seeking to get his model right.

We will start at Aylesbury and work our way along the line to Cheddington, later exploring the traffic on the Branch and the people who worked on and near it. Much of Geoff's research was used to help Bill Simpson's excellent book *The Aylesbury Railway* which remains the definitive history of the line. This part is illustrated mainly using Geoff's own original sketches and photographs as well as some supplied by many other people over the years. Study of his sketches will reveal the extreme detail that he sometimes included. At times he would give talks on his model and appeal for information and he also sometimes placed adverts in local newspapers appealing for help.

The chance meeting with George Thorne in the goods yard in 1957 was the start of the collection of a vast amount of information over the next forty years. George had a very good memory of the Branch going back to before WW1 and produced the first early photograph of himself standing beside his passenger guard's van in Aylesbury station in about 1912. From this Geoff was able to also obtain photographs taken before WW1 by Billy Sutton who had been a porter at the time – surely few porters would have owned a camera in 1912 so this was the start of some of the luck Geoff had on his quest for information.

George Thorne, who was passenger guard on the branch until its closure to passenger traffic in 1953, seen *c.*1912 at Aylesbury. Much of the research on the branch is thanks to George.

Billy Sutton, Porter

The start of the model was of course the track and this was based on Ordnance Survey track plans, but there were naturally differences over time so he plumped for the 25 inch 1925 version assuming it had been surveyed a few years earlier [it had been revised in 1923]. Some details would be confirmed in time by period photographs but other details came from the many friends Geoff built up over the years. For example, Ned Goodyear, signalman at Aylesbury for many years, recalled that when a race special arrived hauled by a Precursor 4-4-0 the engine was too long to fit at the stops near the Park Street level crossing on the passenger run round so that was how

Geoff built the model! George Thorne also remembered that the LNWR basket works, replaced by the council yard in the 1930s, was approached by a cart way leading from the main running line immediately on the Aylesbury side of the Park Street level crossing, so that the buffer stop was not up against the Park Street fence, another feature Geoff had to model. Many similar clues were picked up in this way, such as George Thorne recalling that eight horse boxes would fit in the 'middle road', the siding in front of the main platform, which was not obvious from a small scale OS map.

BUFFER STOPS AND GROUNDFRAME

Another feature that was difficult to get right were buffer stops. In later days most were LNWR-pattern rail-built with the odd timber stops, sometimes earth-filled. To try to get back to pre-WWI days a little detective work was sometimes required. Reg Devereux, a local coal merchant, remembered that at the end of the platform ramp was a lever frame on a raised platform but during a shunting incident it was demolished when a wagon went through the wooden stops at the end of the siding. Geoff had only seen a rail-built stop and the ground level lever frame that replaced it and had assumed they were original. A rating plan showed that the two coal sidings behind the platform fence ended in a double timber buffer stop but it was also Reg Devereux who confirmed that the drawing was wrong and that each siding had separate stops at the end. George Thorne was adamant that originally (to him – c.1912) all buffer stops were timber. By the 1950s the buffer stops at the end of the platform were also rail-built but George assured Geoff that this too was originally timber and later research showed holes in the end wall of the station where the timber buffer stop had been.

Plan and sketch of original station raised ground frame from meeting with George Thorne in December 1960.

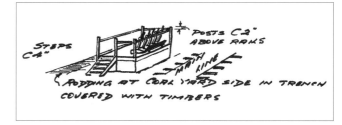

Sketch of original station raised ground frame from meeting with Reg Devereux, November 1960.

LMS replacement of the original timber buffer stop at the end of the platform, set forward a little from the station end wall.

Platform Stops. Replacement of original L.N.W. type

The timber 'middle road' buffer stop showing the raking struts housed into the front wall and showing similar holes where the platform road stops had been before being replaced with a rail-built buffer stop.

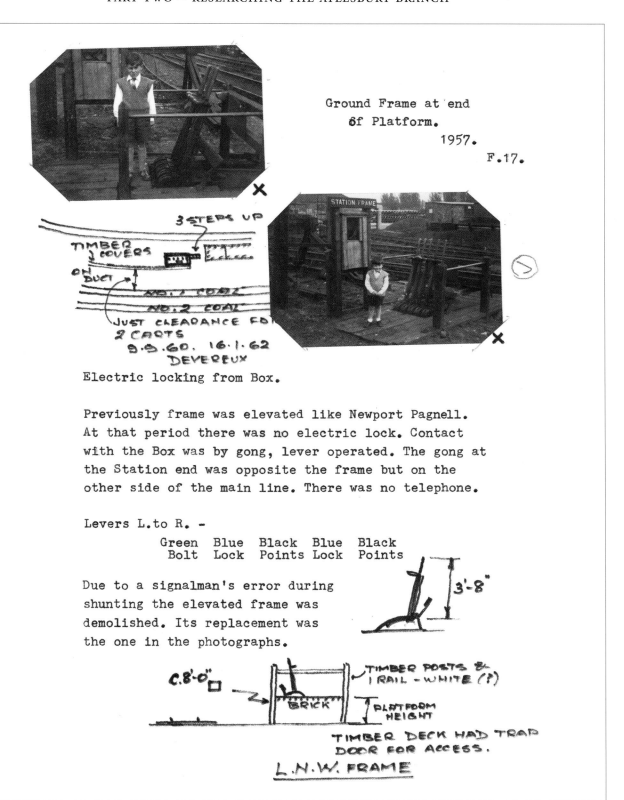

Ground Frame at end
6f Platform.
1957.
F.17.

3 STEPS UP
TIMBER COVERS
ON DUCT
NO.1 COAL
NO.2 COAL
JUST CLEARANCE FOR 2 CARTS
9.9.60. 16.1.62
DEVEREUX

Electric locking from Box.

Previously frame was elevated like Newport Pagnell.
At that period there was no electric lock. Contact
with the Box was by gong, lever operated. The gong at
the Station end was opposite the frame but on the
other side of the main line. There was no telephone.

Levers L. to R. -
        Green   Blue   Black   Blue   Black
        Bolt   Lock   Points Lock   Points

Due to a signalman's error during
shunting the elevated frame was
demolished. Its replacement was
the one in the photographs.

3'-8"

C.8'-0"□
"BRICK"

TIMBER POSTS & 1 RAIL - WHITE (?)
PLATFORM HEIGHT
TIMBER DECK HAD TRAP DOOR FOR ACCESS.
L.N.W. FRAME

Geoff's notes for the station ground frame in 1957 as rebuilt after a shunting incident. The original had been elevated like that at Newport Pagnell. Neither had electrical locking and communication with the signal box was by use of a gong, the station one being on a post the other side of the passenger run round. Author top left, younger brother Pete right.

11'-0"

30"×30"

11×11×¾"dia.
HOLES

1956

Replacement after
accident during
shunting,butoriginal
6f this type.

1957

The station water column in 1956/57. This had replaced the original, of the same type, after a shunting accident and is shown with the fire devil located in an attempt to stop the water freezing in cold weather.

Aylesbury station from near the gas works wall in the 1950s. The timber milk landing had been replaced by then and the allotments once tended along the back of the station had been long overgrown. The line of poplar trees were along Lover's Walk which ran along the railway boundary. The two buffer stops are on Nos. 1 and 2 coal sidings and replaced two earlier timber-built stops.
Source unrecorded

PLATFORMS

With the track work in place the next job was the platform. Being built as late as 1889 it was soon clear that the original had not been altered in either length or height and that the brickwork beneath, and the large stones on top, shown in a photograph of George Thorne taken by Billy Sutton in 1912 were also as-built. However, Geoff still had to make detailed notes and sketches of these features to be able to model them accurately. He soon learnt that it was particularly important to note the colour of things as colours seem to be notoriously hard for people to remember. He noted that the concrete milk landing built behind the platform at the end of the station building did not look that old in the 1950s and discussion with George Thorne revealed it was originally a timber structure with steps at one end instead of the concrete ramp. Geoff sketched it as per George's description and made the model to suit. One can appreciate his relief when George later confirmed a photograph of Geoff's model to be correct! Geoff took a lot of trouble to get the platform surface solid, flat and the correct colour realising that once the flower beds, lamps and especially the glass roof and screen were in place it could never be changed. His researches on-site showed that the horse and carriage dock just opposite the platform was a different surface and was actually made of the well known LNWR blue, diamond-pattern engineering bricks. He was always open to accept things may not be as they might be assumed, for example there are very many different types of fence on his model because that was what his researches showed. No using a typical proprietary model fencing!

Right: The well-tended garden and rockery of whitewashed stones opposite the platform near the horse and carriage dock *c.*1912. The fence along the back marks Lovers' Walk. *Billy Sutton, Porter*

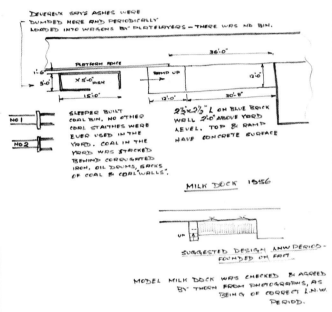

Plan of milk dock area in 1956 and suggested previous timber milk dock from descriptions as later confirmed by George Thorne.

THE STATION BUILDING AND GLASS SCREEN

The next area for attention was the station building. The station building is largely straightforward although the roofing is more complicated but the station glass roof and screen proved much more of a challenge. Geoff set about this by taking several photos from all angles and by making many very detailed dimensioned sketches. Without the ability to go up on the roof the higher parts were measured by counting the number of standard LNWR bricks. The architecture was generally very similar to Rugby station which helped. Later he was fortunate to come across an official drawing of the station building, but historical colours and materials had still to be worked out. Again the memories of George Thorne helped along with Arthur Clark. In some places Geoff's research went into even more detail, recording aspects which would never be used in the model purely because he had found them. One example of this was that when cast iron plates had been removed from some of the doors they revealed painted wood graining (scumble) beneath, which even memories from 1912 could not recall. This was probably from when the station opened in 1889 although no living memories went back far enough to confirm. He also removed a small section of wallpaper from the booking hall which had been revealed and which nobody could remember, this too perhaps going back to 1889 or soon thereafter. The colour and pattern of floor tiles in the gents' toilets were recorded (red and yellow!) although of course they would not feature in the model.

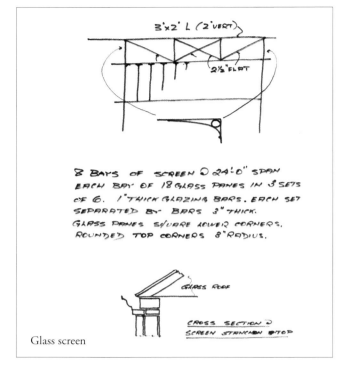

Glass screen

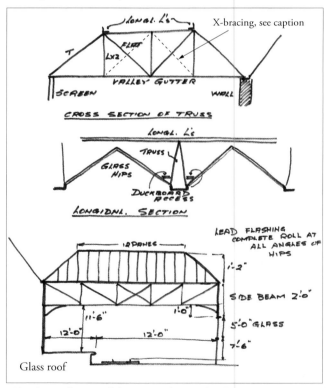

Glass roof

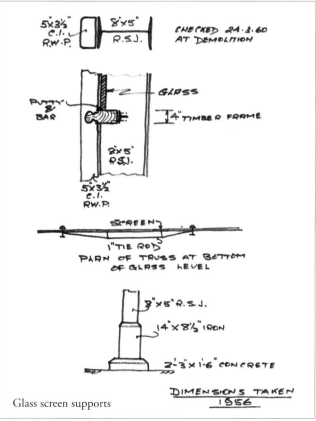

Glass screen supports

Sketches and notes of the station glass roof and screen (surveyed and drawn 1956 to 1960 before demolition). Geoff's survey was carried out from ground level with the result that the main roof truss (upper left) hidden above the obscure and dirty glass was initially drawn with single braces. By the time Geoff came to build the model he had obtained official drawings which showed the correct double X-bracing.

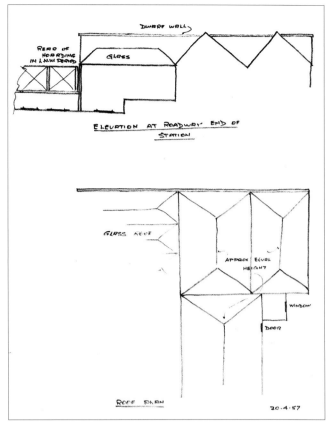

Arrangement of roof, drawn in 1957.

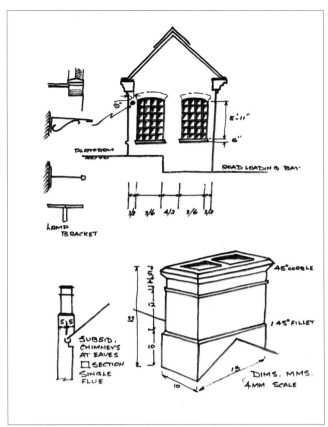

Construction of the end of the station building and chimneys.

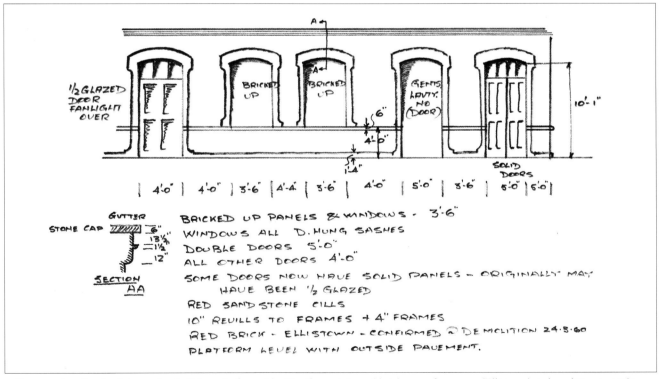

Construction details of the station building platform side. Geoff noted the red brick manufacturer as 'Ellistown' at demolition in 1960.

AYLESBURY STATION (LNWR)

Drawing based on official LNWR drawing 'New passenger station for Aylesbury' dated 1888.

Scale of this reproduction 2mm : 1ft.

Drawing by S. Phillips

SLATE

— **PART WEST ELEVATION** —

BOOKING HALL

PARCELS

GENERAL WAITING ROOM

LADIES 3rd CL WAITING ROC

— **EAST ELEVATION** —

Note: All the lower halves of windows facing platform except General Waiting, Gentlemens Waiting Room & Booking Hall to have ground glass. All windows to WCs to be glazed wholly of ground glass.

3" RWP

3" RWP

RWP

BOOKING OFFICE

BOOKING HALL

PARCELS OFFICE

GENERAL WAITING ROOM

LADIES 3rd CLASS WAITING ROOM

RWP

RWP

P   L   A

8' 0"

EXTENT OF SMOKE BOX

24' 0"

— **PLAN** —

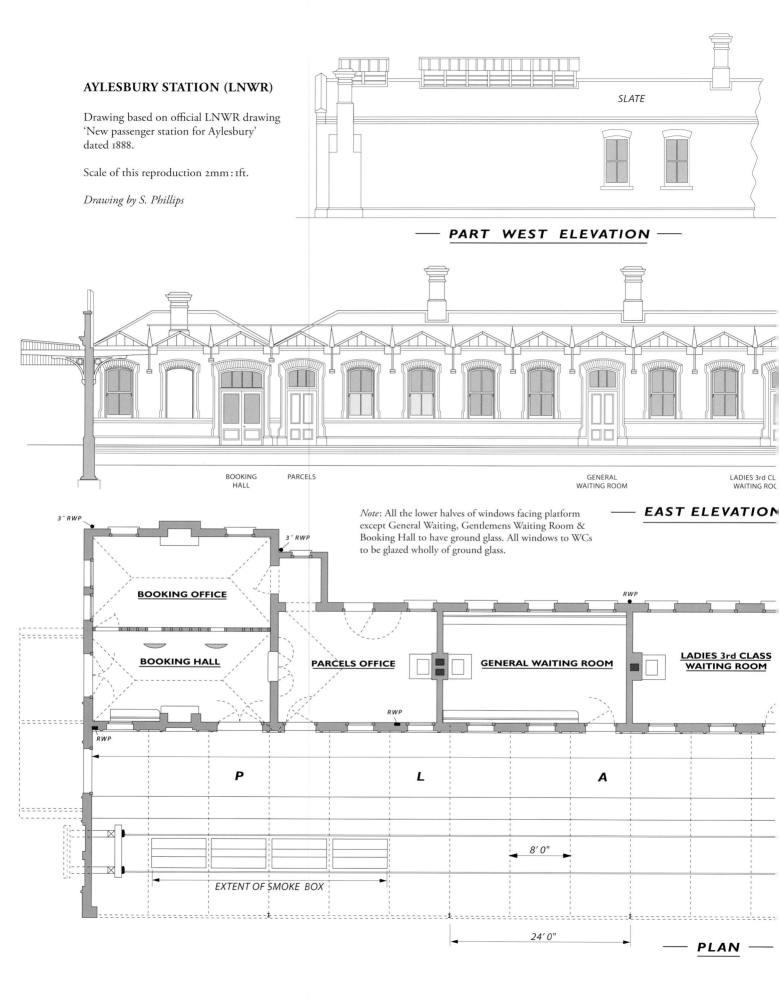

SLATE

Note:
North, East & South Elevation of
Booking Office to be faced with
pressed bricks. The screen wall at
end of platform to be faced on both
sides with red pressed bricks.
The west elevation with exception
of booking office to be faced with
picked bricks. The whole of the
foundation walls to have a damp
proof course of tar asphalt.

— PART WEST ELEVATION —

20' 6"   6' 0"

LADIES 1st/2nd CLASS
WAITING ROOM

GENTS 1st CLASS   PORTERS   STORES
WAITING ROOM

GENTS   BOILER
TOILET   ROOM

(PLATFORM) —

10   5   0   10   20   30   40   50 FEET

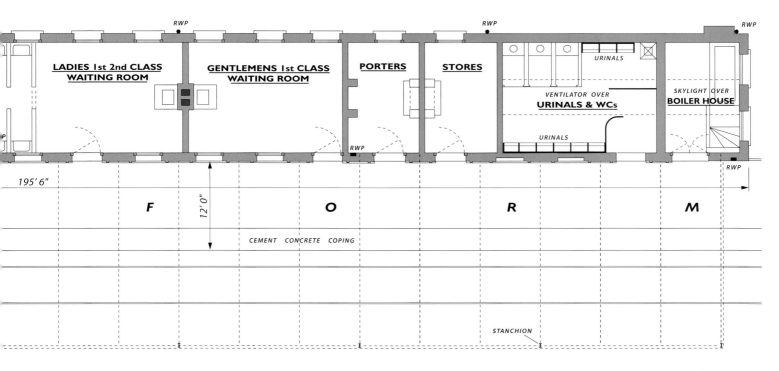

RWP   RWP   RWP

LADIES 1st 2nd CLASS   GENTLEMENS 1st CLASS   PORTERS   STORES   URINALS   SKYLIGHT OVER
WAITING ROOM   WAITING ROOM   BOILER HOUSE

VENTILATOR OVER
URINALS & WCs

RWP   URINALS

RWP

195' 6"

12' 0"

F   O   R   M

CEMENT CONCRETE COPING

STANCHION

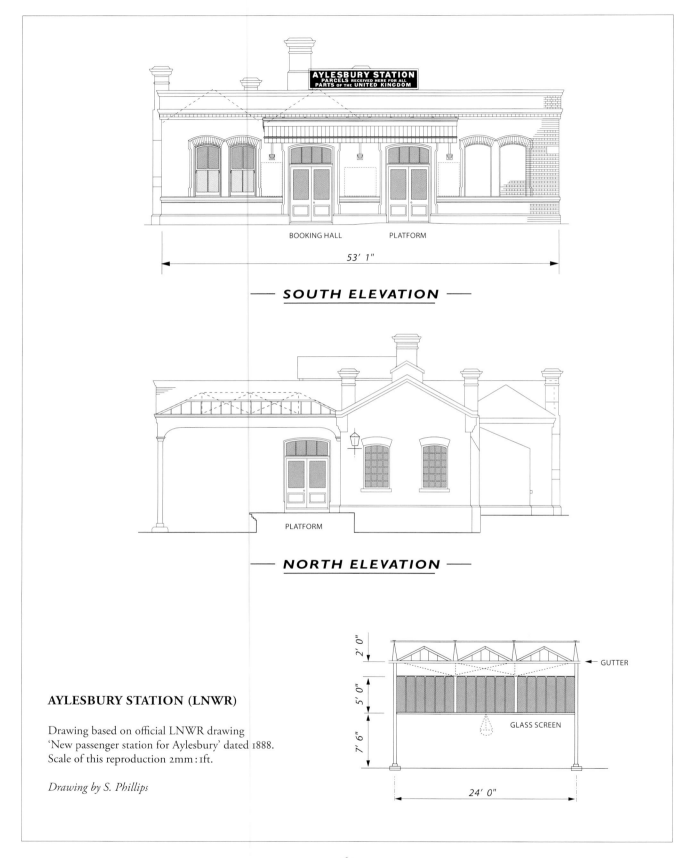

AYLESBURY STATION
PARCELS RECEIVED HERE FOR ALL
PARTS OF THE UNITED KINGDOM

BOOKING HALL   PLATFORM

53' 1"

— SOUTH ELEVATION —

PLATFORM

— NORTH ELEVATION —

AYLESBURY STATION (LNWR)

Drawing based on official LNWR drawing
'New passenger station for Aylesbury' dated 1888.
Scale of this reproduction 2mm:1ft.

Drawing by S. Phillips

2' 0"

5' 0"

7' 6"

◄— GUTTER

GLASS SCREEN

24' 0"

Geoff's photograph of the west elevation *c.*1956 showing neglected former allotments. The weighbridge office is seen to the right.

Above: The east elevation of the station building under the glass roof. The prototype was built with pressed red brick, very precisely laid to English bond and Geoff captured the character of the building through careful observation and recording of the prototype before it was demolished in the early 1960s.

Left: The west elevation of the station building was rarely photographed. Although not seen from the front of the layout, Geoff modelled it fully. The area between the building and the roadway was used for allotments which were abandoned and overgrown when Geoff surveyed the building. In the distance is the weighbridge office. *Colour photographs by Andy York, BRM magazine*

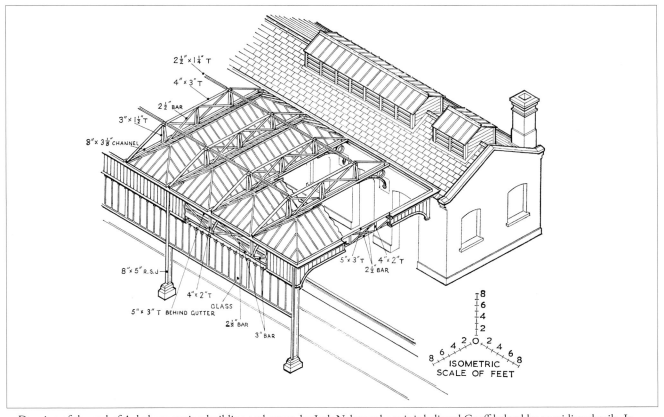

Drawing of the end of Aylesbury station building and screen by Jack Nelson whom it is believed Geoff helped by providing details. It was included in *LNWR Portrayed* by Jack Nelson, Page 130, Fig 11-28 published in 1975. *Courtesy Peco Publications*

Said to date from *c.*1910 this photo shows much useful detail including the glass roof and screen with supporting ironwork and smoke hoods, also station signs, lamps and adverts. The van on the left is a 26ft brake van converted for milk traffic use. It is interesting that there are no flower beds around the screen stanchions or hanging baskets at this period.

Courtesy Leicester Museum

George Thorne had already given Geoff a photograph of himself standing on the Aylesbury platform in 1912 which showed a hanging flower basket from the station screen in the background. Soon he was given several more of Billy Sutton's pre-WW1 photos showing details of flower beds in many other places. These included around all the glass screen stanchions, along the platform outside the station, around the station front fence and even off the end of the horse landing opposite the platform. These gave enough details to see the whitewashed stone borders and the sizes of the plants, although the actual plants could not be identified. What a colourful sight they must have been – and this was when the station was already over twenty years old. It is interesting to note that the photograph from Leicester Museum (see previous page) looking along the platform reputedly in 1910 shows no flower beds or hanging baskets and this is a mystery that has not been resolved. Billy Sutton's few photographs also provided a lot of other useful information on the platform including the position of station seats, the design of the original station lamps (long gone when Geoff first arrived there), station adverts and especially the high close-boarded station fence, replaced by a shorter open paling design by the 1950s. George Thorne remembered there were

two station nameboards along the platform, two seats and three flower beds. As usual Geoff recorded all colours where possible although features like window frames and station fences were assumed to conform to LNWR standard pre-group colours.

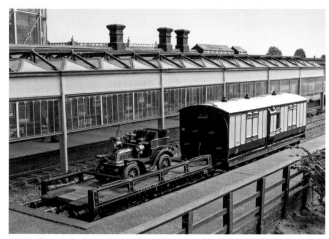

Geoff modelled the screen with hanging baskets and flower borders as shown in period photos taken by porter Billy Sutton.
Photograph by Andy York, BRM magazine

Looking along the platform line in 1956, three years after passenger services on the branch had ended and shortly after Geoff had first discovered the station. The surviving LNWR period details made the station an attractive subject for a model. *Geoff Williams*

A sample of wallpaper found in the booking hall in the 1960s. Traces of similar paper were found in other rooms too and wood graining was found on some doors beneath the cast iron door signs but all this was beyond the memories back to 1910 and may have been original in 1889.

Rare pre-1914 photograph of the screen with a line of horse boxes in the horse and carriage dock. Note that the flower beds and hanging baskets are flourishing at this time. The distinctive North and Randall building can just be seen in the distance. Note the bracing to the lower edge of the glass screen.

Billy Sutton, Porter

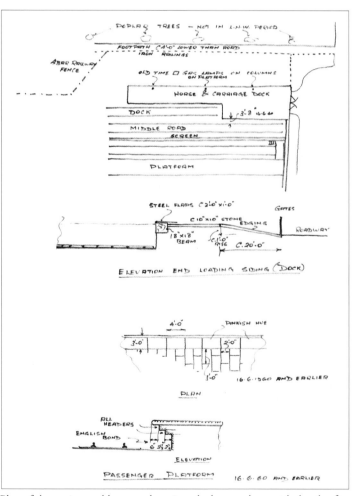

Plan of the station and horse and carriage dock area, along with details of the carriage dock end loading ramp and the main station platform in 1960.

69

Looking towards the station *c.*1930 there was much to replicate on the model. Note the horse boxes in the horse and carriage siding, the LNWR ground signal and point lever, the old station lamps and the earlier and taller close-boarded platform fence with serrated top. There appear to be gardens or allotments on the left and certainly milk churns on the platform near the milk dock.   (*LGRP 11723*)

Looking towards the station after 25th September 1950 when the station was renamed 'Aylesbury High Street' and new signs were erected. The old station lamps were still in place but the point lever has changed for the LMS type, the platform fence is the lower, open paling type and the milk dock gates near the building had gone. Note also the 'new' line of poplar trees along Lover's Walk.   (*LGRP 24785*)

Sometimes features shown in some of these pre-WW1 photos could be linked and explained. For example there was a wooden walkway across the back of the buffer stop in the platform with steps leading down to ballast level but seeing the flower beds, hanging baskets and the ground signal just inside the screen made it clear that this was to allow access for maintenance. It was George Thorne who explained that the ground signal acted as a calling-on signal for backing out a train from the platform while the shorter lower arm on the post near the council yard just off the end of the platform was actually a repeater for this. This knowledge helped ensure they were placed in the correct position on the model. In December 1959 as parts of the line were being demolished the two-arm signal including the calling-on arm was cut down and a friend, John Edmunds of the HMRS, rescued the shorter arm and delivered it to Geoff's house in Cheshunt. His family still treasure it.

The starter and calling-on signal on 28th January 1959. It was demolished in December that year, by cutting through the post at ground level, but the shorter calling-on arm was saved by John Edmunds (of Aylesbury) and delivered to Geoff's home in early January 1960.

Aylesbury passenger calling-on arm as preserved at Geoff's family home in Cheshunt.

ALLOTMENTS

Several early photos from various sources showed allotments on land that was totally overgrown when Geoff first saw it and this reflected a different way of life when people grew their own produce and many allotments beside railways were run by railway employees. Gradually one-time allotments were identified opposite the platform near the station (from 'Billy Sutton' photo), behind the station building alongside the entrance to the coal yard (per George Thorne), as well as several areas beside the line on the way to Cheddington. All these were discovered thanks to photographs or discussion with people who ran them.

The end of the station building in 1956, looking across from the remains of some of the many allotments that had at one time been tended at many locations around the station. The unfenced platform area near the station building shows the location of the milk landing. Note the dominance of the gas holder which is not yet in its fullest position.

71

THE HIGH STREET

At first the entrance to the main station in High Street was a mystery but soon photos emerged both from the station side by Billy Sutton and from the road side. It was fortunate that the professional photographic business of Mr and Mrs Payne was run from a house in High Street almost opposite the station and several photographs were eventually collected showing details of fences, signs, flower beds, etc. The High Street buildings themselves had to be researched for the model and some of them belonged to North and Randall, mineral water manufacturers just opposite the station. Mr Cooper, the Managing Director of the business in 1972 was most helpful in helping to track the building layout in earlier times. One persistent query in High Street however, was the colour of the street lamps. This seemed to change over time and eventually Peter Barnett, a family relation who had been county librarian at Aylesbury, helped with information that the posts were green and cream in pre-WWI days.

Right: Once the track was lifted and the building demolished it wasn't long before nature took over as shown in this photograph taken of Beryl in 1965. The view looks towards the High Street, with North & Randall's building to the left near the trees.

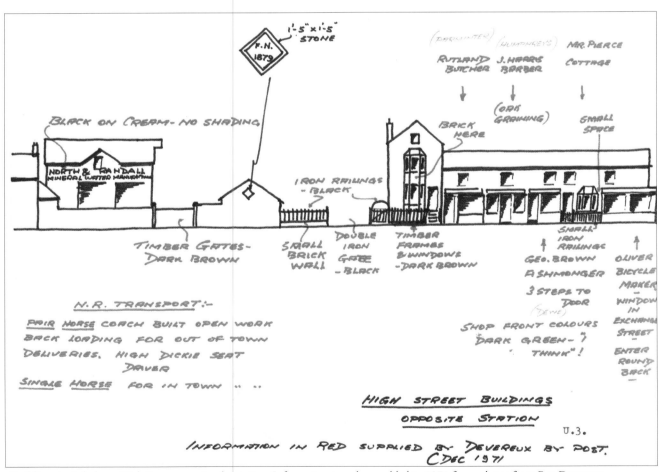

Buildings in Aylesbury High Street opposite the station. Information in red was added in 1971 from a letter from Reg Devereux.

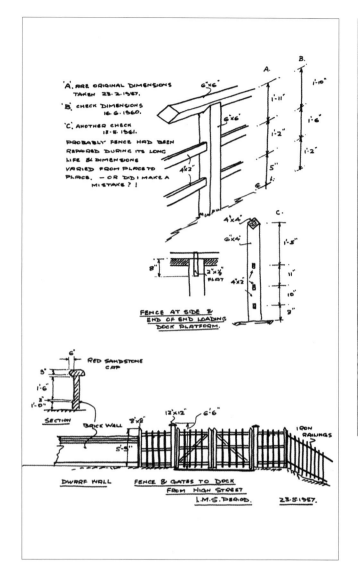

Arthur Clark pre-1914 showing the station forecourt side of the station fence on Aylesbury High Street, also giving details of the rockery, nameboard, saw-tooth fence, etc. *Billy Sutton, Porter*

Left: The fence along the side of the horse and carriage dock, the fence and gates along the front giving access from High Street and the dwarf wall from that fencing across to the station building (surveyed and drawn 1957 to 1961).

Composite photograph of buildings on the opposite side of Aylesbury High Street taken in 1957. The distinctive outline of the cream-painted North and Randall building, so clearly visible from the station, can just be seen due to the oblique angle.

Aylesbury station looking across High Street *c.*1910. The closed gates to the left of the station entrance form the entrance to the gas works. Note the period details of fencing, nameboards, adverts, lamps, etc. *Courtesy Leicester Museum*

Photo taken from the first floor of the Chandos Hotel and looking along High Street, then still known as New Road, in the direction of Tring. It is believed the occasion was the visit of General French and the Squadron of Lancers in 1912. *Commercial post card*

PLATFORM FURNITURE AND LAMPS

Platform furniture was another feature that had to be pieced together from several sources and eventually it was found that the usual standard LNWR seats were used and pensioners who had used the line as employees or passengers helped build the picture of how many there were and where they were placed. When Geoff first found the station the platform lamps were of the four-sided tapered type but George Thorne and others described hanging glass bowls with a top that lifted off. Some of the original cast iron posts were still in place, and Geoff even removed one of these but it was some time before evidence surfaced to confirm the true design of the lamps themselves. They were then identified as a standard LNWR design and the mystery was solved.

Looking along the platform pre-1914 with the taller, close-boarded fence and with plenty of enamel adverts. Note also the original lamps, flower beds (with roses?) and typical LNWR station seat.

Billy Sutton, Porter

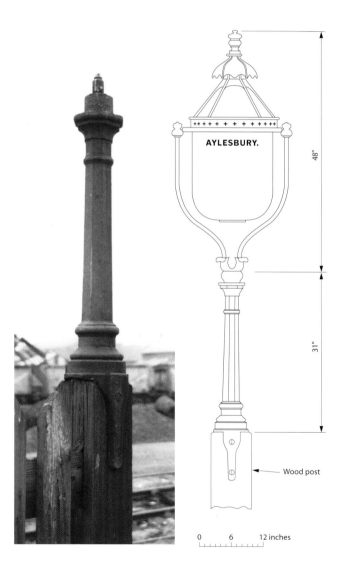

The standard LNWR cast iron lamp post was moved from the earlier close-boarded fence to the newer fence. Photographed on 23rd March 1960. *Photo Geoff Williams, drawing S. Phillips*

Close up of lamp under the glass roof. The design was the same as used on the platform fence albeit with the support yoke mounted on a cast iron post. Note that the glass bowl is lettered AYLESBURY.

Just three years after closure to passenger traffic, all signage has been removed from the station and the forecourt is being used as a general car park. Geoff's beige Morris Minor, 195 GMU, is parked on the far left.

Below: A period view of a yard full of Nestlé-liveried Albion A10 lorries of the type built from *c.*1910 and reputedly used to carry milk between the Nestlé factory and High Street station. This photo formed the basis of a model of one of the lorries.

Source not recorded

OSIERS AND THE LNWR BASKET WORKS

From 1880 the main LNWR basket works, making mail baskets, hampers and carrying baskets for most of the system, was located in Park Street on the south side of the railway. It produced baskets until 1947, although locally-grown osiers were only used up to about 1930. The main material for basket making was cane from coppiced willow plants (osiers) grown along the south side of the line from Park Street back to the station itself but also along much of the rest of the line. A representation of osier plants is included on the model along the front of the baseboard as well as bundles of cane ready for taking into the basket works. Around twenty men were employed at the works and also cutting osiers along the line.

MILK DOCK

Just off the end of the platform was a short siding that older memories described as where milk vans were loaded with Nestlé's milk from their local Aylesbury factory. Later a photograph was found showing the Nestlé-liveried Albion lorries used at the time and one of these was modelled. Another pre-1923 photograph showed Dominion Butter being loaded into a LNWR van at the platform and correspondence with Jim Richards revealed exactly the type of van used so that too could be modelled. Very much later the use of Aylesbury LNWR station was confirmed as the despatch station for Dominion butter when a Dominion butter invoice was acquired, thus tying the story together.

LNWR refreshment hamper, a product of the LNWR basket works in Aylesbury
Mike Williams

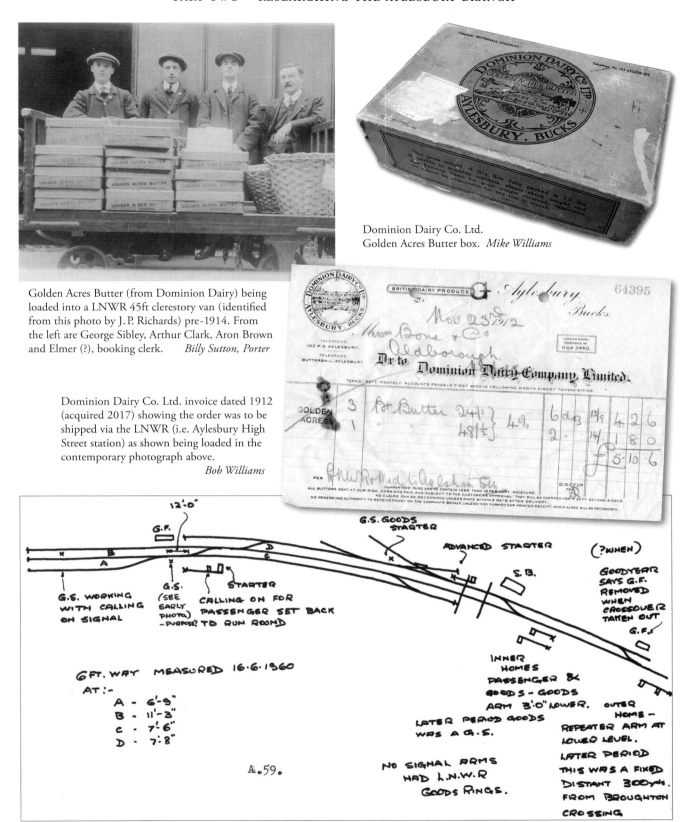

Dominion Dairy Co. Ltd.
Golden Acres Butter box. *Mike Williams*

Golden Acres Butter (from Dominion Dairy) being loaded into a LNWR 45ft clerestory van (identified from this photo by J. P. Richards) pre-1914. From the left are George Sibley, Arthur Clark, Aron Brown and Elmer (?), booking clerk. *Billy Sutton, Porter*

Dominion Dairy Co. Ltd. invoice dated 1912 (acquired 2017) showing the order was to be shipped via the LNWR (i.e. Aylesbury High Street station) as shown being loaded in the contemporary photograph above.
Bob Williams

Plan of the various station signals drawn with the help of ex-signalman Ned Goodyear. The siding used for loading Nestlé's milk is also shown.

Of course sometimes research unearthed information that could not be included in the model but Geoff still recorded it methodically so nothing was lost. One example was the method of running round passenger trains. According to passenger guards working at Aylesbury at the time, the official way was for the train to be reversed out of the platform and stopped just past the crossover to the carriage dock and middle roads. The loco would then uncouple, drive over the crossover into the middle road, reverse along the run round track beside the basket works (later, council yard) and then join the train over the crossover near the Park Street crossing. However, it was found that whilst the original 1839 station had been almost level, when the new station was opened in 1889 it was down a significant slope. This meant that running round could be (unofficially) simplified by reversing the train out of the platform. The guard would then hold the train on the hand brake while the loco was eased into the middle road and then he could release his brake and let the carriages roll back into the platform under gravity. The loco could then re-join the train.

THE GAS WORKS

The gas works was researched largely from Geoff's own professional knowledge from working for Eastern Gas with some help from Southern Gas, but the usual question of historic colours arose and was very important with structures the size and dominance of the gas holders. Research from many sources produced about seven different colours but of course these structures were there for over sixty years so all were probably correct at different times. A little reasoned logic and guesswork resulted in the final decision to use red oxide on the model.

The coal yard still held considerable stocks of coal in 1957. These are Nos. 1 and 2 coal sidings. Note the retort house has a tall chimney at this date.

The gas manager's house just past the entrance to Aylesbury gas works, as viewed from the entrance road to Aylesbury coal yard in April 1958.

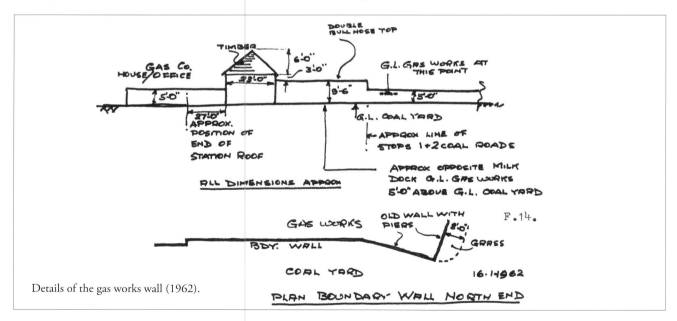

Details of the gas works wall (1962).

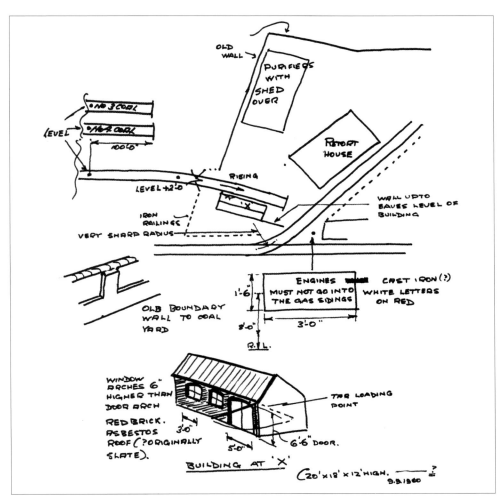

Plan of far end of gas works (1960).

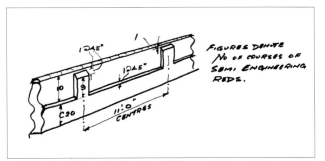

Sketch of gas works wall (1960).

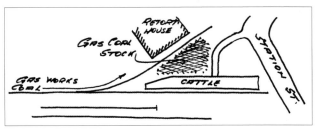

Plan showing location of gas works coal stock from a meeting with George Thorne in December 1960.

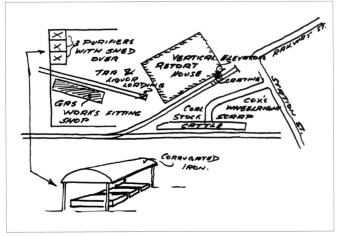

Plan of the far end of the gas works from a meeting in December 1960 with Mr Dorrell who started work at High Street station in 1916.

THE COAL YARD

Working our way along the line from the station the next area for attention was the coal yard. An LMS-period rating plan (see p. 8) established the shape and size of the coal stacks and also where the coal merchants' huts were situated. Discussion with several retired coal merchants (especially East, Hawkins and Devereux) from the post-group period not only provided further detail but also information about wagons used and how they were lettered. Reg Devereux also supplied several photos of the coal yard showing his railway wagons, horse-drawn and petrol lorries. Crucially Reg was also able to remember the elusive details about colours.

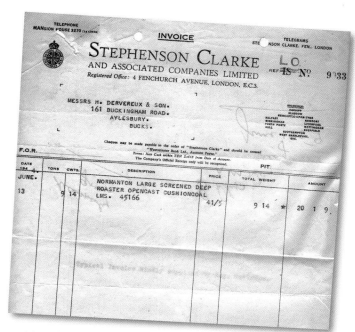

1944 Stephenson Clarke invoice for supply of coal to H. Devereux and Son, accounting for use of Stephenson Clark PO wagons used on the branch. *Reg Devereux*

This 1957 view across the coal yard gives a good view of the backscene to be reproduced on the model. Note the later rail-built buffer stop to the siding, which was at the end of the platform. Road access behind the siding allowed loading of Nestlé milk traffic into bogie vans, of which the siding could accommodate two.

Another 1957 view across the coal yard. The main running line is in the foreground followed by the 'milk siding' and the first two coal sidings. Coal sidings 3 and 4 are behind the coal heaps.

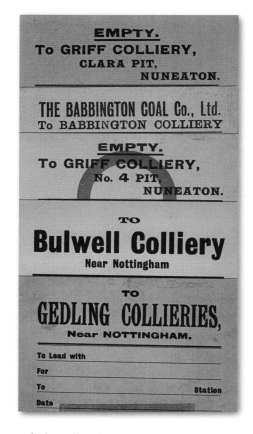

Selection of other colliery labels showing suppliers to H. Devereux and Son and showing PO wagons used on the branch. *Reg Devereux*

Old LMS parcels van No. 36 as purchased by coal merchant Reg Devereux for £1 and photographed in June 1961.

One of Reg Devereux's four coal wagons. This one was purchased second-hand from Friths, Aylesbury timber yard, and retained their No. 11. It was Devereux's only wagon with an end door.
Reg Devereux

One of Devereux's coal trollies. *Reg Devereux*

Devereux's American-made Maxwell motor lorry purchased second hand after WW1 with acetylene lighting and solid tyres. The livery of all Devereux's road vehicles was blue with red wheels and white lettering. The cab appears to be home-made. *Reg Devereux*

Devereux's later motor lorry, although still pre-WW2, fitted with pneumatic tyres. *Reg Devereux*

Below: Devereux's fleet of road vehicles standing against Aylesbury No. 2 coal road unloading coal for Aylesbury Power Station. This photograph gives other useful information like PO wagons from Spenser Whatley and Mapperley and also the neat coal stacks. The presence of vans in No. 1 coal yard was unusual according to Reg. *Reg Devereux*

The coal yard weigh bridge and weigh house in 1957, situated beside the station building at the entrance to the coal yard. Note that the chimney of the office is arranged at an angle.

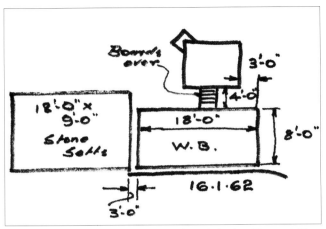

Plan of the coal yard weigh house and weigh bridge (Drawn 16th January 1962).

LOCOMOTIVE SHED

The locomotive shed ('Steam shed' in LNWR parlance) was the next landmark to be seen when travelling towards Cheddington and this, although still standing, had been reduced in length in LMS days with a straight concrete lintel used at the shortened western end in place of the elegant brick arch still surviving at the eastern end. Again the memories of those familiar with the line before Nationalisation said that the roof-mounted water tank latterly situated near one end had originally been in the centre. The shortened version had five panels then one under the water tank and then one more before the 'new' end. Geoff therefore built his model with five panels each end plus one under the tank, making eleven in total. Imagine his frustration when at last in 1980 David Clark gave him a 1935 photo of it showing five panels at one end, one under the tank but then six at the western end making twelve in total. He could not face making a new model so the incorrect one remained. When visiting the site after the shed had been demolished it was found that rails still in situ in the shed area were still supported by very small, possibly original, London and Birmingham Railway chairs.

One of the few known photographs of the original unshortened locomotive shed photographed on 24th November 1935. This view shows the west end and north side elevation. *W. A. Camwell*

The main entrance to the locomotive shed showing original brick arch and the south-facing side elevation on 28th November 1960.

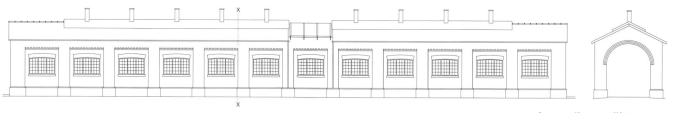

Drawing of the shed in the LNWR period, before the building was cut back to X-X by the LMS.

The far end of the locomotive shed as shortened by the LMS and using a reinforced concrete lintel in place of the earlier style brick arch.

Inside the loco shed looking east on 28th November 1960. Originally there were work benches down one side of the shed which accounts for the track being laid off-centre. After demolition it was found that the rail chairs in the shed were tiny and probably original (London and Birmingham Railway). The rail certainly looks very worn!

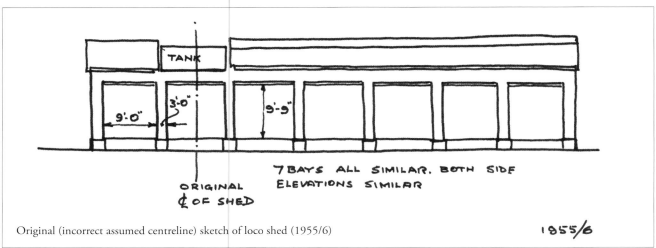

Original (incorrect assumed centreline) sketch of loco shed (1955/6)

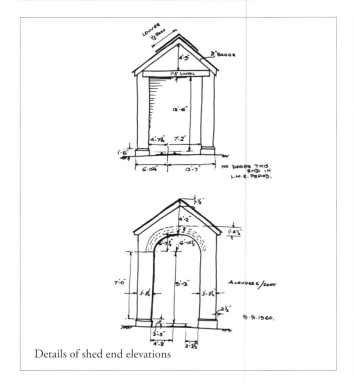

Details of shed end elevations

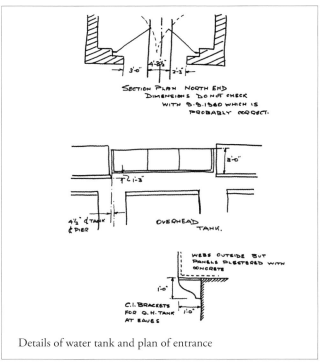

Details of water tank and plan of entrance

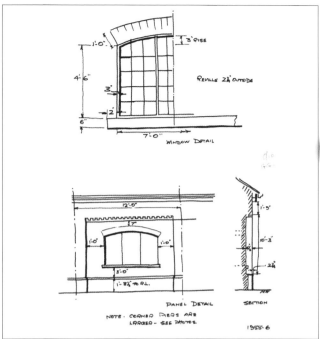

Sketches of loco shed windows and walls (1955 to 1960).

Comparison of chairs. LNWR standard chair behind a chair recovered from inside the the steam shed after closure. Believed to be ex-London & Birmingham, it was still supporting rail. Base of the smaller chair is 10¼ in × 4¾ in.

Photo Mike Williams

GOODS YARD

Whilst exploring around the north side of the locomotive shed the extent of the goods yard became apparent and this started a lot more research. This had been the original passenger station until 1889 and had been developed to include the usual goods yard facilities like a large timber goods shed, a cattle dock (with timber fencing replaced with concrete), an extra siding enter-

ing the gas works as well as end loading, yard cranes, wagon turntables, etc. Fortunately, most of this was still there in the 1950s although largely overgrown. Site measurement and extensive sketching produced a clear enough picture for modelling as this was situated at the far back of the model and could not be seen close up but still considerable detail was recorded.

Aylesbury goods shed viewed from the cattle dock on 28th November 1960. The goods yard access road passed behind it. The significance of the enamel plate No 162 (white on black) is uncertain.

Inside the goods shed on 24th September 1959. The crane was still in place but out of use by then and the shed was rented out to a local spirit merchant.

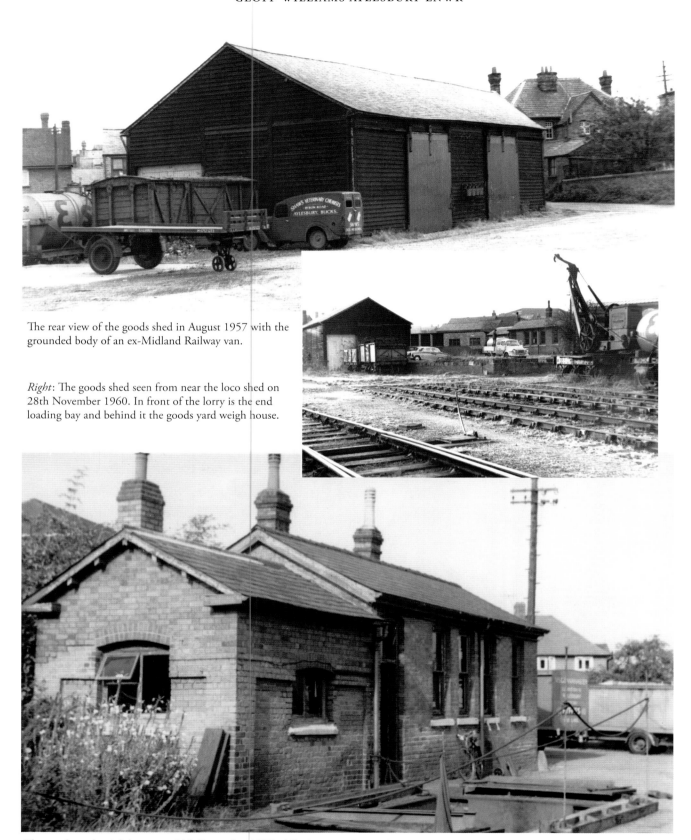

The rear view of the goods shed in August 1957 with the grounded body of an ex-Midland Railway van.

Right: The goods shed seen from near the loco shed on 28th November 1960. In front of the lorry is the end loading bay and behind it the goods yard weigh house.

The goods yard weigh house on 24th September 1959 whilst it was under repair.

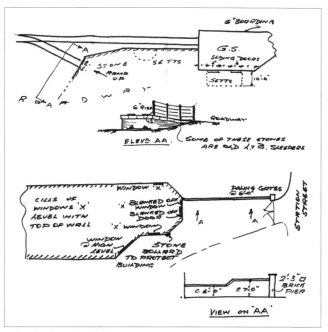

Sketch of goods shed.

The cattle dock.

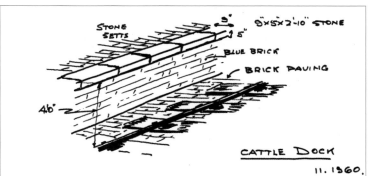

Sketch of cattle dock area.

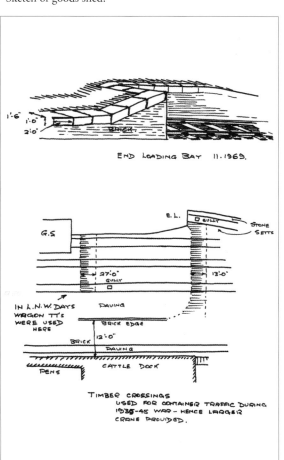

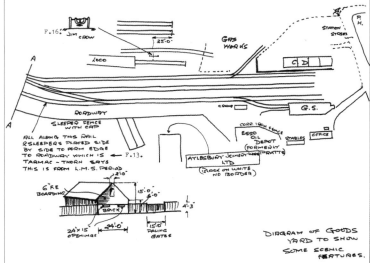

Isometric sketch of goods yard end loading bay and plan of end loading/cattle dock area of goods yard (1969).

Plan of goods yard area with details of buildings and fences off railway property.

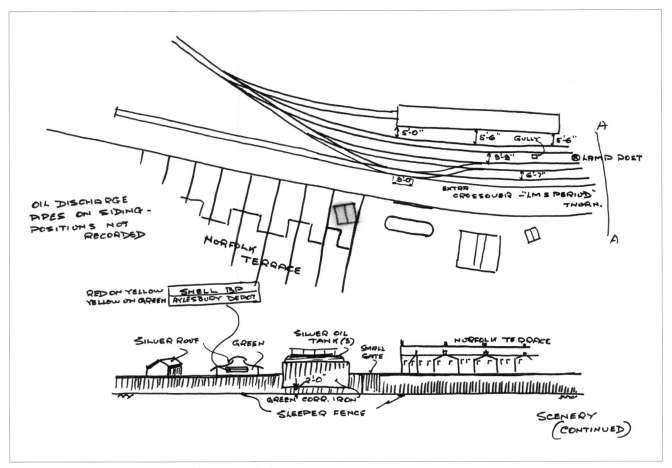

Goods Yard plan showing area behind locomotive shed.

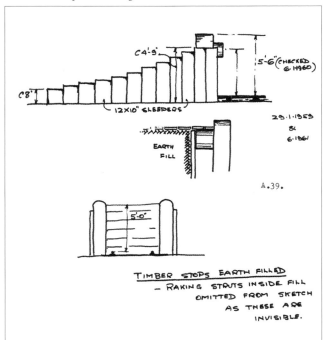

Construction of earth-filled timber buffer stop (1959-1961).

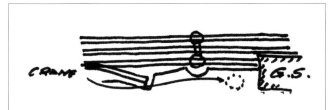

Sketch of goods yard wagon turntables from 1896 rating plan owned by Mr R. W. Fenton from a meeting in December 1960.

Sketch of jim crow stored near the loco shed from meeting with Reg Devereux November 1960.

PART TWO — RESEARCHING THE AYLESBURY BRANCH

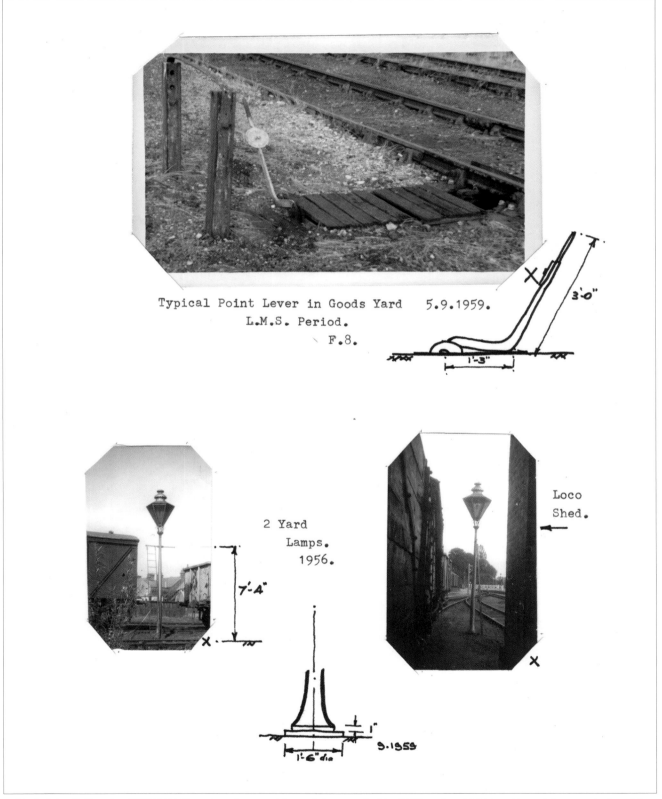

Typical Point Lever in Goods Yard   5.9.1959.
L.M.S. Period.
F.8.

2 Yard
Lamps.
1956.

Loco
Shed.

Typical details found at LNWR/LMS stations: large yard lamps (photographed in 1956) and an LMS signal lever (photographed on 5th September 1959).

89

SIGNALMEN'S COTTAGES

Approaching Park Street crossing the very distinctive signalmen's cottages stood on the northern boundary of railway property as they were in place while the 1839 station was still in use. This property carried two cast iron numberplates, 1049 and 1050, but although most surviving cast iron property plates were lettered L&BR (London & Birmingham Railway) the Aylesbury ones were lettered L&NWR so the building was probably erected after the original station had been in use for some years. Geoff got to know some of the signalmen, one of whom was Ned Goodyear, still living in the cottages, and was able to make quite detailed dimensioned sketches of not just the cottages but also the fences and out-buildings. Lengths could be measured but heights were calculated by counting bricks (four courses to the foot).

One of the original cast iron number plates from Aylesbury signalmen's cottages

Aylesbury signalmen's cottages photographed in September 1958. These pre-date the 1889 station and the oblique alignment follows the line into the original station. There were two semi-detached cottages here and some of Geoff's Aylesbury research was helped by Ned Goodyear who lived in the nearer one in this photo.

Looking towards Park Street from the goods yard on 29th January 1959, the signalmen's cottages are prominent and also the platelayers' hut. By then the signal box had been demolished but the footbridge was still standing. The timber buffer stop was one of the last remaining at Aylesbury.

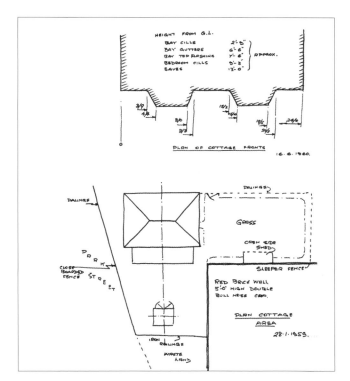

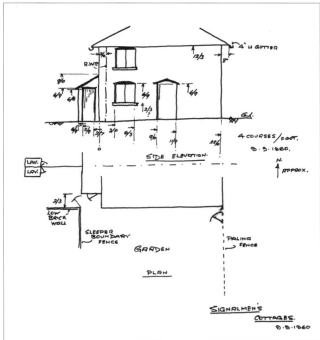

Sketches of signalmen's cottages, gardens and fences (1959 to 1960).

NORFOLK TERRACE

Norfolk Terrace, which still exists at the time of writing, was a road of terraced houses running along the line of the railway boundary fence from Park Street and was towards the loco shed a significant feature that needed to be modelled. Geoff called at some of the houses in Norfolk Terrace and built a picture of which houses had garden sheds, outbuildings etc. The model was slightly less than scale size to allow for perspective but, learning from his experience of finding out the historical colour of things he noted that Norfolk Terrace was made from red brick with light colour pointing and slate roofs.

Norfolk Terrace in 1957.

Some of the most well-known photos of the Aylesbury Branch were taken from the footbridge looking towards Aylesbury and Geoff took one too. It is interesting to study his photo from 1958 with one taken perhaps twenty-eight years earlier and to understand how he had to make adjustments to his notes and observations to try to produce the scene from pre-group days. The first obvious change was the removal of the passenger run round and its crossover back to the mainline but the earlier photo does show that the run round did stop short of Park Street crossing to allow for the sleeper cartway to a gate in the boundary fence (removed in the later photo) to what a few years earlier would have been the LNWR basket works. The replacement council yard and road shows in both photos. The other trackwork change was the removal of the single slip leading to the goods yard. This small change would have had a major operational impact as the short spur of the slip would have allowed an engine to reach virtually any siding

of the entire station without the need to use the level crossing. However, by the time the slip was removed it is possible that engines then in use were too long to use the spur anyway.

On closer inspection there are several other changes like the addition of the three grounded van bodies and the erection of a separate building between the line to the loco shed and goods yard and the siding in front of Norfolk Terrace on the right. It is interesting that the goods starter ground signal has been moved from the left of the above line to the right but also further forward perhaps suggesting that goods trains were being run more from the goods yard. Other features have remained surprisingly unchanged like the oil tank wagon facility at the end of the siding on the far right and the virtually unchanged skyline of Aylesbury town apart from some gas works features. Very careful scrutiny of the roof also reveals the original longer engine shed in the earlier picture.

Looking towards the station from the footbridge, 1930. Many features were new to Geoff when he was given this print by David Ratcliff, particularly the single slip track layout leading to a short spur from which most of the station could be reached without using the level crossing. The LNWR basket works was across the field on the left before its use by the council and the passenger run round timber buffer stop was set back from the level crossing to allow the cart track from the running line to the gate in the fence (still in place in this photo) to allow osiers collected along the line to be taken into the works. The photograph also showed that the tank wagon unloading that Geoff had seen in the 1950s was there in the 1930s. There were also cover timbers and walkways along the track that could be included in the model. The gas works had vertical retorts at that time. (*LGRP 11724*)

Looking towards the station from the footbridge in 1958. Several changes have occurred since the 1930 photo but particularly to the track. The passenger run round has been considerably shortened and its crossover to the mainline removed. Lying on the track bed is the remains of what is probably the same platelayers trolley seen in the 1930 photo. The single slip has been removed to leave just two simple catch points. There are several other changes in the gas works and additional storage has been provided on the right in the form of a large shed for banana ripening and three van bodies, two MR and one LNWR. To the left of the picture is the council depot. Some osiers appear to have survived and are growing near the railway fence.

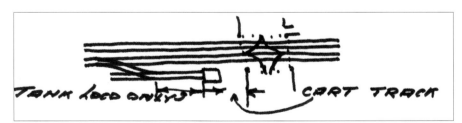

Sketch plan of basket works cart track at Park Street from a meeting with George Thorne in June 1960.

PARK STREET LEVEL CROSSING

We now come to the most complicated part to model: Park Street, its level crossing and the road at right angles to the front of the model baseboard. Apart from the issues of perspective mentioned in Part One there are a lot of features that needed to be researched and understood before the model could be started. From observation Geoff believed that the rows of houses either side of Park Street probably went back to LNWR days but several photos were required to ensure they looked right on the model. Many visits to site and studying several photographs also revealed that around the crossing itself were four different types of fence/railings and these were faithfully reproduced. The scene was complicated because there was no straight curb to the left of Park Street past the signalmen's cottages so the alignment of buildings had to be clearly understood. Jack Tofield, whose Motor Engineers business was on the right just past the crossing, and George Thorne were a help in this area. Geoff would have been excited to have seen the pre-WW1 photo of the crossing, acquired in about 2015 from Mike Sargeant which shows his interpretation of what it would have looked like in LNWR days was generally accurate. The two main 'errors' were the houses in Bierton Road that must have been built later and the – inexplicable – lack of a red disc in the centre of the level crossing gates.

A wonderful photograph looking up Park Street *c.*1910 which, by comparison with the model, shows that Geoff's researches to recreate the scene at about 1910 were quite accurate. Unfortunately this photograph only surfaced about sixteen years after he died. *Mike Sargeant*

Looking up Park Street on 10th June 1959 with the end of Norfolk Terrace just visible on the left.

Another view looking up Park Street towards Bierton Road taken a little further up from the crossing on 24th September 1959.

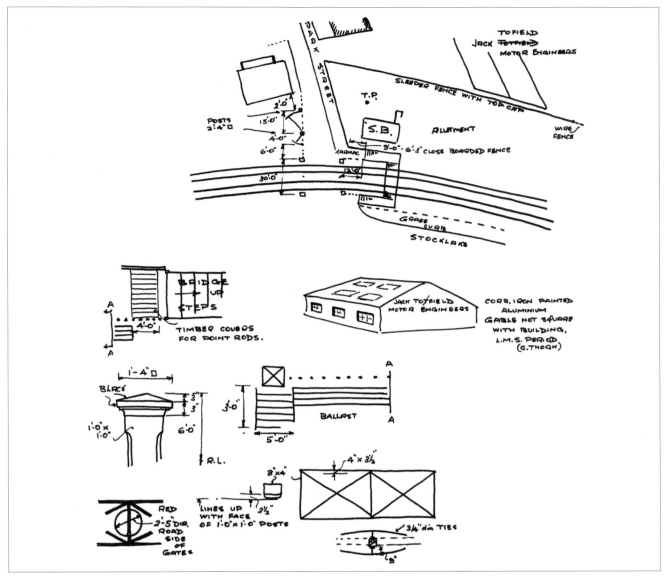

Plan of Park Street crossing area and details of crossing gates.

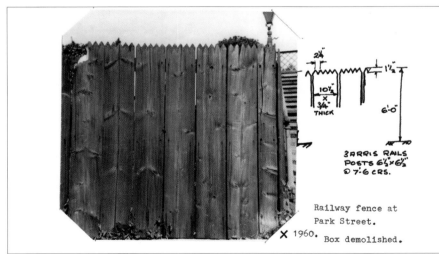

Detail of railway fence in Park Street. Details taken in 1960 after the signal box had been demolished.

AYLESBURY SIGNAL BOX

Signal boxes were generally pretty standardised by WWI but Geoff still did a lot of ground research to ensure he got it right. This entailed more photographs and dimensioned sketches and of course discussion with some of the signalmen like Ned Goodyear who had known it for so long. Research showed that the box had a lavatory to the right of the door originally but this was replaced by a bucket (!) according to George Thorne and had gone completely when Geoff first saw it. The wooden steps had been replaced with steel by the time he saw it too and he also spent time around the back to ensure the coal bin was correct. He was lucky to have examined the box when he did because by 1960 it had gone.

Right: The signal box photographed in April 1958 this view also shows detail of the footbridge. By this date the lavatory at the top of the stairs had long gone and the wooden stairs had been replaced by steel.

The relative positions of the footbridge and signal box are seen here in April 1958 with the decorative fence edging the walkway. Note the signalman's Royal Enfield motorbike.

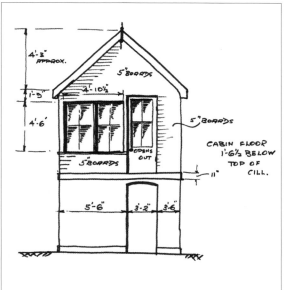

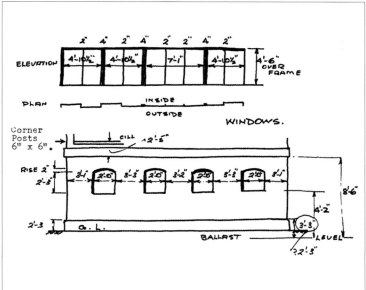

Sketches and dimensions of the signal box, surveyed before the box was demolished in 1960.

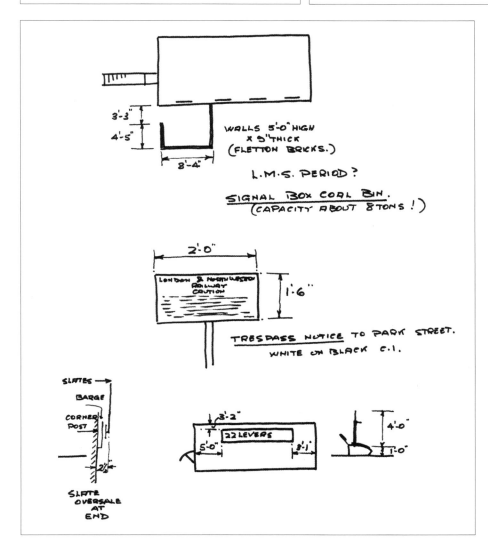

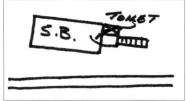

Sketch of original signal box toilet from meeting with George Thorne December 1960.

THE FOOTBRIDGE

Beside the signal box and immediately beyond Park Street crossing was the footbridge, the only bridge on the Aylesbury Branch, erected in 1883 following the accidental death of an elderly man on the crossing in 1880. Fortunately, the bridge seemed to change little over its life, even retaining the lamps on the two landings so historical research was less important here. However, being such a distinctive and complicated structure Geoff made many detailed sketches and took several photographs to make sure he had recorded all the detail he needed in case it was demolished before he could build the model.

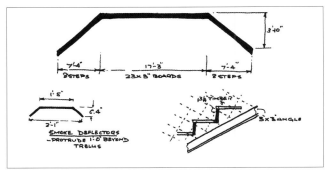

Footbridge survey notes.

Right: View of the south-east corner of the bridge with the signal box in the background in 1958. Note the surviving lamp.

Looking towards Cheddington, a view along the branch beneath the Park Street footbridge in 1957. The lone poplar tree stands out among the chestnut trees lining the railway in this view.

The standard LNWR footbridge seen in September 1958 with Jack Tofield's large Motor Engineer premises behind. George Thorne remembered this building was built during the LMS period and was corrugated iron painted silver. Jack Tofield himself later helped with some research into the branch.

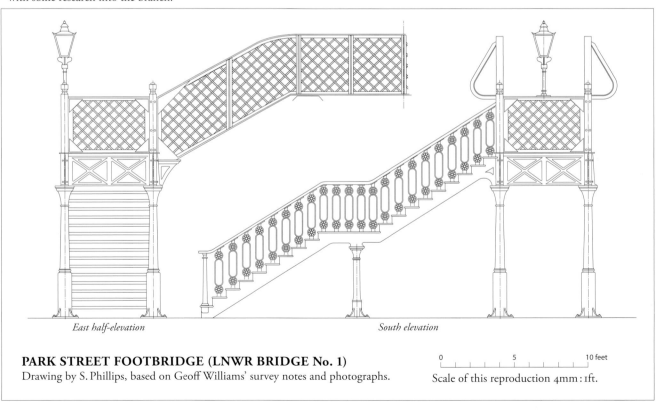

East half-elevation   *South elevation*

PARK STREET FOOTBRIDGE (LNWR BRIDGE No. 1)
Drawing by S. Phillips, based on Geoff Williams' survey notes and photographs.

0   5   10 feet
Scale of this reproduction 4mm : 1ft.

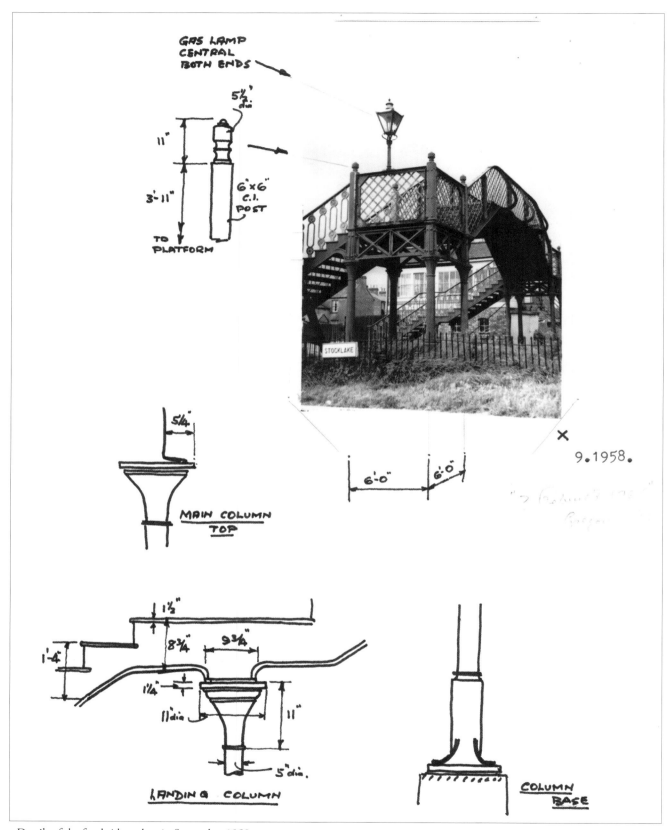

GAS LAMP
CENTRAL
BOTH ENDS

5½' dia

11"

3'-11"

6"×6"
C.I.
POST

TO
PLATFORM

5¼'

MAIN COLUMN
TOP

9.1958.

6'-0"   6'-0"

1½"

1'-4"

8¾"   9¾"

1¼"

11"dia

11"

5"dia.

LANDING COLUMN

COLUMN
BASE

STOCKLAKE

Details of the footbridge taken in September 1958.

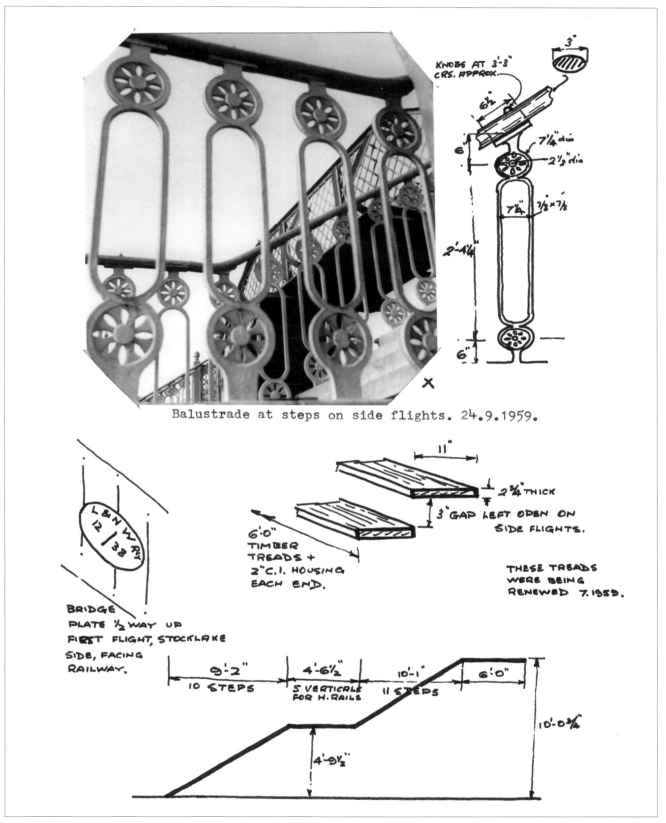

Balustrade at steps on side flights. 24.9.1959.

Detail of the footbridge balustrade taken on 24th September 1959.

HOME AND OUTER HOME SIGNALS

When Geoff first came across the station in the mid-1950s the home signals just the Cheddington side of the crossover to the east of the footbridge consisted of a semaphore for passenger trains and a ground signal for goods about to cross to the goods reception line. George Thorne had described that in LNWR days there had been two separate semaphore signals each on their own separate posts guyed together and, following enquiries through Reg Devereux, Mr H. Scutchings supplied a commercial post card from pre-group days proving that George was right, some three years after he had died, and the model was made accordingly.

Right: View looking east from the footbridge showing the 1950s signalling arrangement when Geoff first saw it. Note the ground signal for goods. Also note the tall poplar tree which Geoff included on the model.

Stock Lake, Aylesbury.

Viewed from the footbridge looking towards Cheddington probably before WW1. The houses on the right lining Stocklake were still there at the time of writing. The main points of interest in this photo are the original passenger and goods home signals on separate posts (the goods signal was soon to be replaced by a ground signal) but the very tall outer home signal with upper and lower arms is also just visible in the background. The train appears to be a Webb 5ft 6in Tank pulling four six-wheeled carriages. George Thorne said the normal branch train consisted of three carriages but that an extra composite was added on market days, stored behind the Cheddington signal box at other times, which this view seems to show. Although, according to George Thorne, tank engines usually ran chimney first into Aylesbury, according to Arthur Waller if a tender engine was used on the branch train it usually worked tender first to Aylesbury in LMS days.

Commercial postcard lent by Mr H. G. Scutchings

It was not just the trains and buildings that warranted Geoff's attention to create the right atmosphere. He even examined the trees and shrubs growing near the line and noticed that the line of trees to the north of the line between the footbridge and the prison were generally chestnuts, with some fruit trees

behind the signal box and these seemed to vary little in photographs of all periods. However, these photos also showed that about the fifth tree from the footbridge was a lone poplar and that too was incorporated into the model.

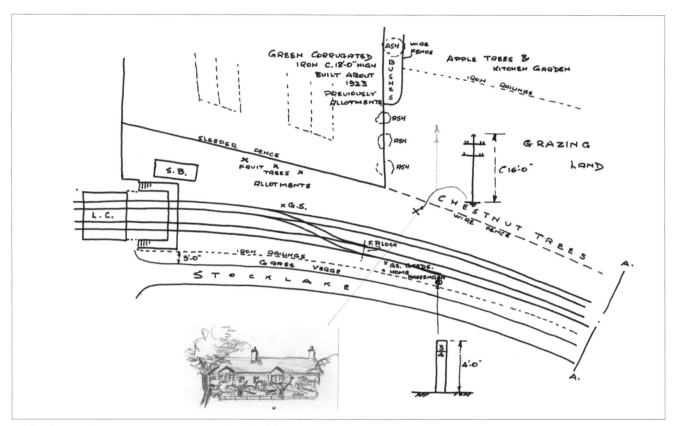

Plan from Park Street crossing to just past the end of the goods headshunt.

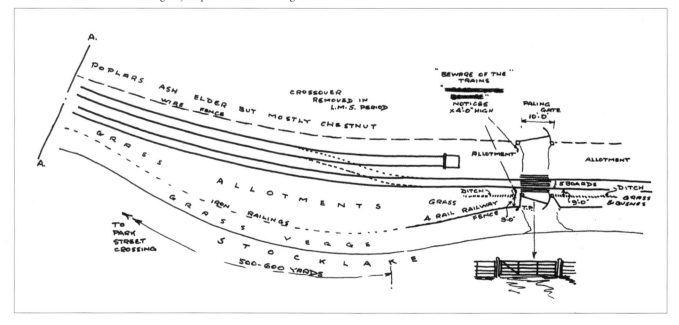

AYLESBURY PRISON

One of the largest structures beside the Aylesbury Branch was Aylesbury prison. Built in 1847 as Aylesbury gaol, it became an adult women's prison in 1890 and was extended in 1895. The entrance to the prison was on Bierton Road which ran parallel to the railway and crossed the west end of Park Street. The prison buildings were not all set parallel to the railway and the red brick architecture was quite complicated. Being a non-railway building Geoff did not consider it worth much research but stood in the 'four foot' of the railway and took a photograph, one of several, which was used as described in Part One. He did later meet prison staff at exhibitions and discussed various aspects of the prison with them.

The siding/headshunt adjacent to Aylesbury prison was known as 'Mrs Maverick's' which is a corruption of the name of American Florence Maybrick who was convicted of murdering her husband in 1889 and was detained in Aylesbury prison, becoming something of a *cause célèbre* until her release in 1904. Suffragette Violet Bland was imprisoned and force-fed during a hunger strike by suffragette inmates there in 1912. She wrote of her experiences in *Votes for Women* and received a medal and commendation from Emmeline Pankhurst. HMP Aylesbury is a Grade II listed building and still operates as a Young Offenders Institution (for 17 to 21 year olds) with a capacity of 444 detainees.

One of several views of Aylesbury prison taken by Geoff in 1958 to form the basis of the backscene on the model.

There was an occupation crossing immediately the Cheddington side of the end of the siding from the footbridge which was duly modelled but further along the line Stocklake swung away from the railway and there was another occupation crossing. Although this was right at the end of the scenic part of the model and baseboard width prevented it being modelled in full he still took a photograph and made a detailed sketch of it.

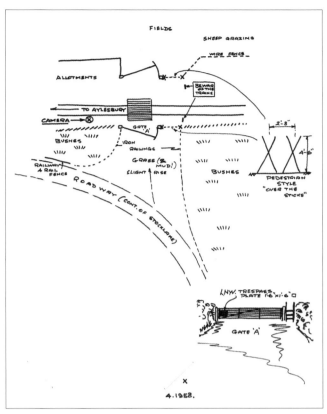

Plan of occupation crossing at the end of Stocklake, April 1958.

The occupation crossing where Stocklake finally veers away from the railway line before Broughton Crossing, photographed in April 1958.

All along the line thought was given to what non-railway features would be visible from the line that would require putting into a backscene, either low relief or painted. Geoff took many photos of such areas and several details can be seen in the background of other photographs and sketches in this book but here are some more.

St Mary's Parish Church features on the skyline just behind the station. George Thorne sang in the choir for many years and his funeral was held there on 9th December 1960.

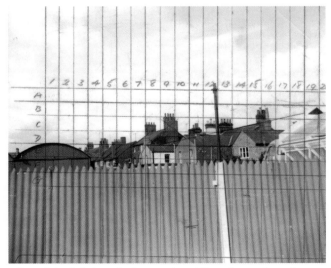

Part of the Aylesbury backscene viewed from the goods yard across the oil depot in 1970. The grid drawn over the photograph was to enable Geoff to replicate the scene, and the perspective on the model backscene.

View from Stocklake on 10th June 1959 across the railway towards Bierton Road showing fields with chestnut trees, taken to enable a realistic backscene to be applied to the model.

The occupation crossing across the line located immediately the Cheddington side of the end of the goods headshunt taken on 10th June 1959.

Considering the LNWR and LMS both made extensive use of motor-fitted or push-pull trains it may seem surprising that none were ever used on the Aylesbury Branch pre-WW2. According to passenger guard George Thorne, this was because the branch engine was used for shunting at both ends of the line and push-pull was only tried later as goods traffic began to fall off. However, according to Jack Turner who worked on the branch in the late '40s and early '50s, it was first tried in 1950 but not for long as the last passenger train just three years later was not push-pull fitted. Both ex-LNWR Webb 5ft 6in Tanks and Ivatt 2-6-2 Class 2 Tanks were used for such trains.

Another feature of branch working which would not be seen on the model but could be built into operating it was goods traffic for Marston Gate. Trains approached Marston Gate from Cheddington over a facing point so any goods traffic for Marston Gate was taken through to Aylesbury and shunted into the Marston Gate siding on the return trip, usually from the front of the train but sometimes from the rear when it was barred into the siding by hand.

Geoff's model finished less than a mile from the Aylesbury terminus but his researches always included the whole branch from Aylesbury to Cheddington and he still took many photographs and made many sketches of features along the rest of the line. Much of this was incorporated into Bill Simpson's excellent book on the branch but some of these are included here for completeness, although he never intended to model more than Aylesbury itself.

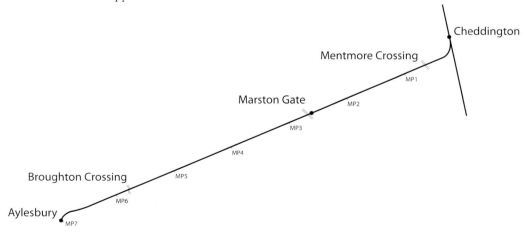

Marston Gate

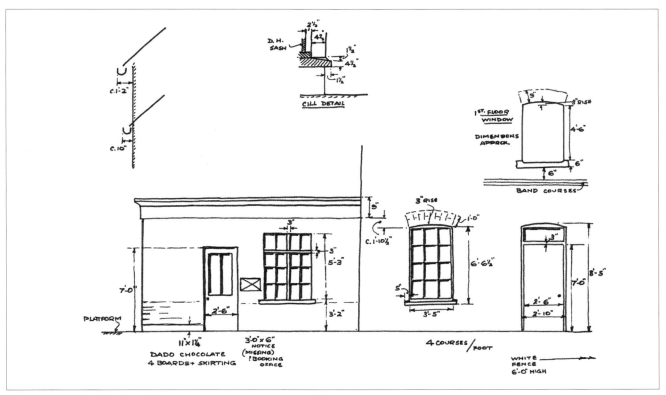

Marston Gate station building details.

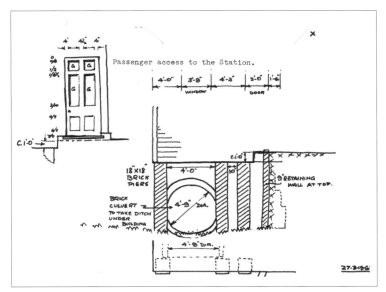

Marston Gate station building end. Details of door and culvert running beneath building (1962).

Marston Gate timber platforms support and platform fence (1962).

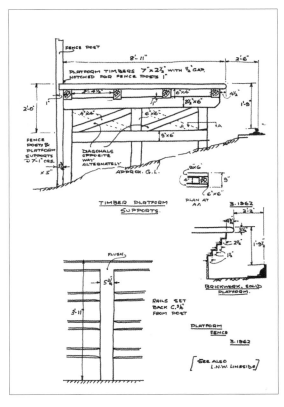

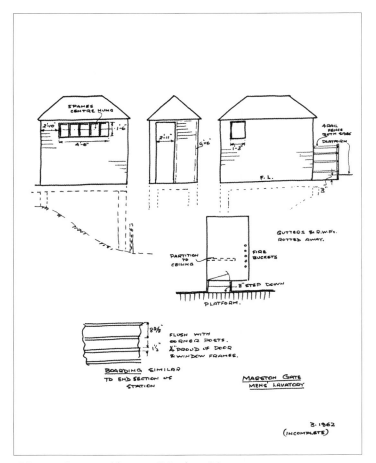

Marston Gate mens' lavatory (March 1962).

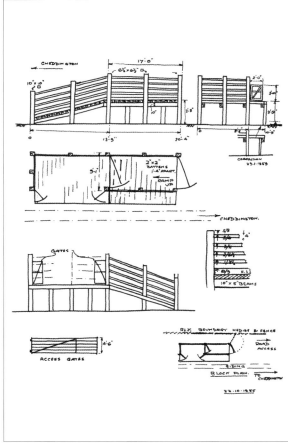

Marston Gate cattle dock (October 1955).

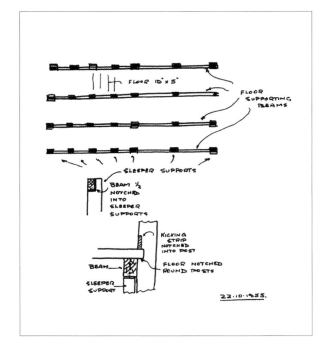

Marston Gate cattle dock (October 1955).

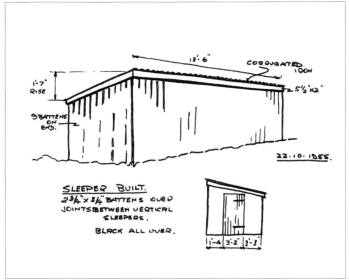

Marston Gate coal hut (October 1955).

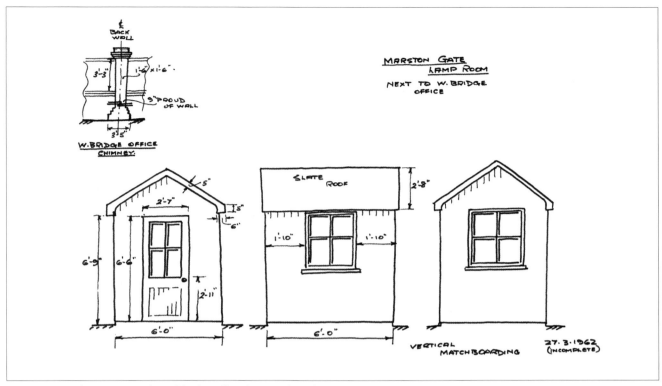

Marston Gate lamp room and weighbridge office chimney (March 1962).

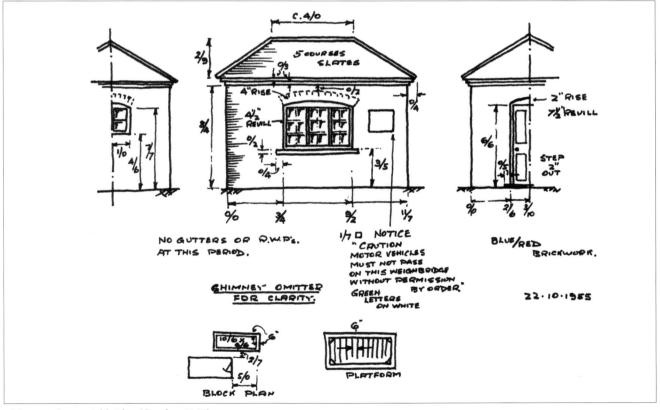

Marston Gate weighbridge (October 1955).

Marston Gate station from the
goods yard on 27th March 1962.

Marston Gate station from the
road on 27th March 1962.
The ditch runs underneath the
building on the left side.

Marston Gate cattle dock on 29th January 1959. Note how the access gate seals off entry to the yard beyond when open for cattle.

Marston Gate timber platform supports on 27th March 1962.

Timber gents' lavatory on 27th March 1962.

Marston Gate coal store on 29th January 1959.

Marston Gate weigh house with weigh bridge in front and timber lamp hut beyond on 29th January 1959.

Mentmore Crossing

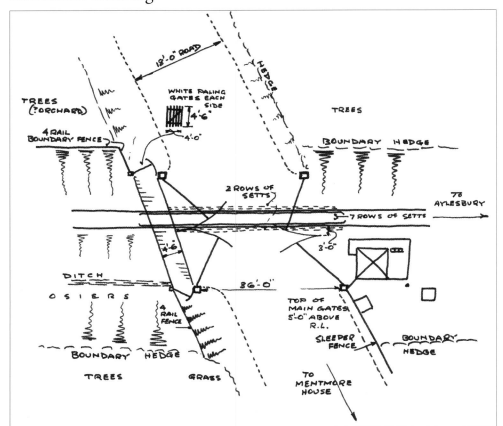

Plan of Mentmore
Crossing area.

Plan and elevation sketches
of Mentmore Crossing hut.

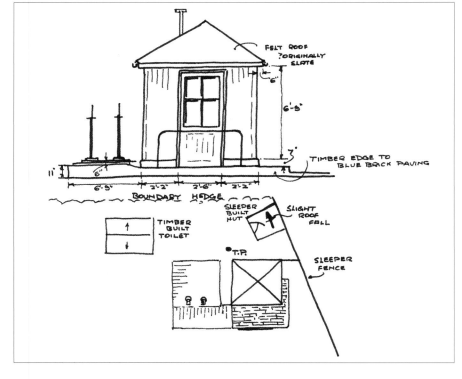

Mentmore Crossing looking towards Cheddington in September 1957. Note the unusual layout of the name, in screwed iron letters, arranged either side of the door.

Cheddington

Cheddington station looking north from the Aylesbury platform in April 1963. The footbridge had had its roof removed by then.

Cheddington station in April 1963 with the Aylesbury platform curving round to the right.

Looking towards Aylesbury at Cheddington station on 15th February 1960 as a Fairburn 2-6-4 Tank shunts thirty-two wagons from Aylesbury.

The view from the brake van of a goods train travelling to Aylesbury on 11th April 1962. This view was the same for most of the seven miles of the branch, a similar photo in Bill Simpson's book being taken a few miles away. Geoff and son Bob had hitched a ride from Marston Gate on the goods train, hauled by Ivatt Tank No. 84004, and then walked back.

Sources used by Geoff for Aylesbury Branch research

Mr Peter Barnett – family relation. Was county librarian at Aylesbury 1950s-60s.

Mr Batchelor – met in 1973 at Aylesbury exhibition. He lived at Edinburgh Place, Aylesbury. Elderly ex-prison officer from Aylesbury prison.

Mr Bateman – met in 1960. He was born c.1887 and had LNWR-employed relatives but never worked for the railway company himself.

Mr Mike Bentley – supplied some photos of the Branch.

Mr Arthur Clark – met in 1959. Arthur was passenger porter at Aylesbury LNWR from 1912, returning there after fighting in the war and retired in the late 1950s.

Mr David Clark – LNWR Society. Supplied photos of the Branch.

Mr Clements – met through LNWR Society c.1975.

Mr R. E. Cooper – met in 1972, he was the Managing Director of North & Randall in High Street, Aylesbury.

Mr Reg Devereux – lived at Buckingham Road, Aylesbury – met from 1959. Reg was a local coal merchant using High Street station for his business and retired in 1959. He then bought a Myford ML7 lathe and built a model steam traction engine.

Mr Ernie Dodd – met 1959. At the time he was shedmaster at Bletchley.

Mr Dorrell – met in 1959. He had started working at High Street station in 1916 and was later a clerk at Aylesbury Town station.

Mr H. East – supplied some photos of private owner wagons.

Mr John Edmunds – HMRS – responsible for rescuing the starter signal arm for Geoff from Aylesbury when the station was demolished.

Mr Fellows – met in 1973 as a pensioner at Aylesbury exhibition. He had been a milkman with a yard in Park Street.

Mr Fenton – met in 1959. He had worked as a clerk in the Aylesbury goods office.

Mr Mike Fox – lived in Swansea – supplied details of Branch private owner wagons. He also built a 7mm scale model of Marston Gate station.

Mr Ned Goodyear – lived in the signalmen's cottages, Park Street, Aylesbury – met from c.1960. Ned had been crossing keeper at Marston Gate before WW1 but was later signalman at Aylesbury for thirty-five years.

Mr A. E. (Sam) Grigg – met in 1970s. He had been a driver at Bletchley shed and supplied some photos of the Branch.

Mr W. J. Hawkins – lived at Tring Road, Aylesbury – met in 1959. He had been a coal merchant at High Street station but had moved on to other work.

Mr Reg Hubbard –ran a corner shop at the junction of Park Street and Stocklake – met in 1959.

Mr Harry Jack – lived in Dundas Street, Edinburgh – met c.1986 via LNWR Society.

Mr Len Kinchen – lived at Sunny Bank, Cheddington – met from 1959. Len was signalman at Cheddington between c.1954 and 1960s until he was made redundant and joined the ambulance service. For a long time his family were friends.

Mr Peter Matthews – HMRS – supplied details of private owner wagons from the Branch.

Mr Philip Millard – HMRS and LNWR Society member. He supplied some original LMS documentation concerning the Branch.

Mr K. A. C. R. Nunn – supplied some photos of the Branch.

Mr Osterfield – historian resident of Aylesbury – supplied some photos.

Mr Hayward Parrott – lived in Church Street, Aylesbury and later Ascott Street. A local historian who responded to Geoff's appeal for information in the *Bucks Herald* in 1959.

Mr Tom Pocock – met 1959-1960. Tom was a platelayer on the Branch.

Mr David Ratcliff – lived in Wembley Park and later near Church Stretton. Met via the HMRS c.1960 where he was librarian. He built a fine model of Banbury LNWR and became a close family friend until his death in the late 1990s.

Mr Robinson – met in 1973 at Aylesbury exhibition. He (or Mr Wheatley) had been a fireman on the Branch.

Mr Jack Rogers – lived at Marston Gate – met from 1959. Jack was crossing keeper at Marston Gate for over forty years. He was born locally although he had worked his way across Canada when he was younger. He had rejected suggestions he should apply for promotion to other stations.

Mr H. G. Scutchings – met 1963 – lived in Eastern Street, Aylesbury. He supplied some Branch photos.

Mr Bill Simpson – met several times over many years. Bill supplied some photos of the Branch and also authored the book on the Aylesbury Branch making much use of Geoff's photographs, drawings and researches.

Mrs Vivien Thompson – met in early 1960s. Vivien was a 4mm LBSC modeller living in St Albans.

Mr George Thorne – lived in Chiltern Street, Aylesbury – from meeting in Aylesbury coal yard in 1957. George started work at Aylesbury LNWR in the bookstall whilst too young for railway service. He was a passenger guard on the Branch from c.1910 until 1953 when he transferred to Aylesbury Town station.

Mr Jack Tofield – ran a garage near Park Street.

Mr Jack Turner – lived at Park Street, Aylesbury – met from 1959. Jack had been a fireman on the branch when starting work in the late 1940s and moved into signalling and later management. He wrote his life story in c.2014.

Mr Arthur Waller – lived in Park Street, Aylesbury – met from 1959. Arthur started as a cleaner at Bletchley during WW1 and was a driver on the branch until 1953. He also had allotments near the loading dock at High Street station.

Mr Laurie Ward – HMRS – supplied some photos.

Mr A. J. Watson – met in 1973. He had been a driver on the Branch in LMS days.

Mr Wheatley – met in 1973 at Aylesbury exhibition. He (or Mr Robinson) had been a fireman on the Branch.

An employee of R. P. Richards, Aylesbury timber merchant (name not recorded) – met in 1959.

'Harold' – met 1958. Harold had been a porter at Cheddington station and was introduced to Geoff by Len Kinchen.

'Uncle' – met in 1973. Introduced by Len Kinchen. He had been a platelayer on the Branch in LNWR days.

Railway Magazine – various issues including 1952 article on the Branch by Clinker.

Bucks Advertiser and *Railway News* – 1953.

Railway Observer – 1950.

SLS Journal – 1953.

Bucks Herald – various issues.

LNWR and LMS publications.

Leighton Buzzard Observer.

Rating Plans.

Ordnance Survey maps.

Patent Office.

Public Record Office, Kew.

Southern Gas Board.

Railway World 1971.

LNWR Society – photos and other information.

Visitors to Geoff Williams' Aylesbury EM at Cuffley

Geoff regretted not keeping a visitors book but the following (incomplete) list has been compiled from known records.

Atkinson, Sandy		Lowe, Mary	LNWRS
Bannister, Keith	HMRS	Lowery, Dave	LNWRS
Barlow, Bob		Lyster, Tony	
Bentley, Mike	LNWRS	Meanley, Bob	LNWRS
Bishop, Peter	LNWRS	Millard, Philip	LNWRS
Bland, Mike	LNWRS	Monaghan, Brian	Photographer
Brace, Dave	School friend	Morgan, Ken	North London Group
Bray, Eddie	LNWRS	Moss, Eric	Neighbour
Bridges, Dennis		Nicholson, John	Bob's neighbour
Burton, David	S4 Society	Nix, Dennis	LNWRS
Carpenter, Roger		Norman, Barry	*MRJ* photography
Catton, David	5516	Osmond, Tony	North London Group
Clarke, David	LNWRS	Patrick, David	LNWRS
Cordell, Dick		Pearsall, John	LNWRS
Cottle, Ken	5516	Peascod, Mike	North London Group
Croall, Sandy	LNWRS	Pennington, David	LNWRS
Dale, Brian		Pinnock, Danny	5516
Davidson, Roger		Pusey, Ian	HMRS
Davis, Peter	LNWRS	Ratcliff, David	Friend
Dowley, Paul	LNWRS	Redrup, John	North London Group
Dowley, Francis	LNWRS	Reed, Colin	LNWRS
Driscoll, Derek	Mike – school	Rhodes, Alan	5516
Duffell, Chris	5516	Rice, Iain	with Bob Barlow
Elkin, Roger	LNWRS	Richards, Jim	Friend
Ellis, Peter	LNWRS	Rogers, Brian	5516
Essery, Bob	HMRS	Rouet, Paul	LNWRS
Everett, Ray	Neighbour	Rowe, J. N. P. (Joe)	5516
Fairhurst, Doug	EMGS	Sapte, Peter	
Foster, Richard	LNWRS	Schofield, Laurie	
Fountain, Simon	LNWRS	Schoon, Ed	HMRS (with Jim Stevens)
Ganderton, Dick	5516	Shaw, John	
Gillam, Tony	LNWRS	Sheffield, Tony	S4 Society
Goodall, Keith		Shelley, John	LNWRS
Gough, Terry		Simmerson, Peter	HMRS
Gowers, John		Simpson, Bill	Friend
Greaves, Chris		Smith, Derek	5516
Hammond, Ray	Neighbour	Stanton, Peter	LNWRS
Harris, Ken	Work friend	Stevens, Jim	HMRS
Hodson, Ray		Taylor, Clive	LNWRS
Hughes, Tim	LNWRS	Thompson, Vivien	HMRS
Hull, Aiden	LNWRS	Thomson, Roy	LNWRS
Hutchins, John	5516	Turville, Peter	LNWRS
Ibbott, Bill		Underwood, Colin	HMRS
Jack, Harry	LNWRS	Waite, Colin & father	5516
Jackson, Peter	Norway	Ward, Laurie	
Jenkinson, David	HMRS	Watling, John	HMRS
Jennison, John	S4 Society	Watts, Tony	5516
Jones, Ken	HMRS/LNWRS	Webb, Brian	5516
Kelley, Philip J.	*MRN* photographer	White, Clive	
Kinchen, Len	Friend (Cheddington)	Wilkinson, Jol	North London Group
Koerner, George	USA	Williams, John	Family
Lacey, Ralph	HMRS	Wood, Ken	LNWRS
Lee, Norman	LNWRS	Woodhead, Ken	HMRS
Lowe, Andy	LNWRS	York, Ken	North London Group

Locomotives known to have visited Aylesbury

The following have been positively identified as running on the branch although many other classes will also have been used. It is believed that no diesel ever visited Aylesbury.

Pre-1923

Aylesbury Railway 2-2-0
London and Birmingham Railway 2-2-0
London and Birmingham Railway 0-4-0
McConnell 0-4-2 Tank
Samson 2-4-0
Webb 2-4-2 5ft 6in Tank
Webb 2-4-2 4ft 6in Tank
Webb 0-6-2 Coal Tank
Webb 2-4-0 Chopper Tank
Webb 0-6-0 Coal Engine
Webb 0-6-2 Coal Tank (No. 1054, now preserved)
Ramsbottom 0-6-0 DX
Webb 0-6-0 Cauliflower

LMS days

Webb 2-4-2 5ft 6in Tank
Webb 0-6-2 Coal Tank
Webb 0-6-2 Watford Tank
Webb 2-4-2 4ft 6in Tank
Webb 0-6-0 Coal Engine
Webb 0-6-0 Cauliflower
Webb 2-4-0 Waterloo (Engineer Watford)
Whale 4-4-0 Precursor
Bowen Cooke 4-6-0 Prince of Wales
L&YR 0-6-0
LMS 4-4-0 Compound
Hughes 2-6-0 Crab
Fowler 0-6-0 4F
Ivatt Class 3 2-6-0
Stanier 2-6-0
Ivatt Class 2 2-6-2 Tank

BR days

Webb 2-4-2 5ft 6in Tank
(including last passenger train in 1953)
Webb 0-6-2 Coal Tank
Webb 0-6-2 Watford Tank
LMS 4-4-0 Compound
Hughes 2-6-0 Crab
LNWR 0-8-0 Super D
Stanier 2-8-0 8F
Fowler 0-6-0 3F
Fowler 0-6-0 4F
Fowler 4-4-0 2P
(including one on post-closure special)
Stanier 0-4-4 Tank (on post-closure special)
Ivatt Class 3 2-6-0
Stanier 2-6-0
Stanier 4-6-0 Black Five
(including last goods train in1963)
Ivatt Class 2 2-6-2 Tank
BR Standard Class 2 2-6-2 Tank
BR Standard Class 4 2-6-4 Tank
Fairburn 2-6-4 Tank
(including one on post-closure special)
Stanier 4-6-0 Jubilee
Fowler 4-6-0 Patriot

INDEX